What We Can Learn
from Faithful Congregations

THRIVING CHURCH

ERIN CASH
KORY WILCOXSON

Praise for *Thriving Church*

This book is a "must-read" as we imagine the church for the twenty-first century. Critical to the life of the church is refuting the age-old and problematic ABCs of church - attendance, building and cash as measures of a thriving congregation. Thriving churches are dynamic regardless of congregational size, campus acreage or liquid assets. *Thriving Church* is a gift for the present and future of the church.

> —Rev. Dr. Karen Georgia Thompson, General Minister and President, United Church of Christ

This book is not a "how to become" a thriving church, but it is "this is what is possible" when thoughtful, spirit-filled clergy and laity give attention to the church in faithfulness to the needs of a congregation and community. Simply put, the questions for discussion and reflection invite movement toward thriving.

> —Rev. Dr. Charisse L. Gillett, President of Lexington Theological Seminary

To weave together creative storytelling with a framework for how to understand thriving congregations is a powerful tapestry of possibility for the future of God's people. Cash and Wilcoxson thread together a diverse set of congregational stories and settings to help us begin to imagine a new way forward in congregational ministry. They demonstrate that the Holy Spirit is present in settings far and wide, brimming with the hope that God is making all things new, including how we inhabit the world as the body of Christ. This book is a masterpiece of God's rhythm for transformation and inspires what can be if we listen for God's movement among us.

> —Rev. Dr. Chad Abbott, Conference Minister, Indiana Kentucky Conference, United Church of Christ and author of *Incline Your Ear: Cultivating Spiritual Awakening in Congregations*

Thriving Church isn't just research—it's a roadmap for faithful leadership. Cash and Wilcoxson share the lived wisdom and bold, honest stories of congregations navigating the complexities of church life with courage and love. Their stories breathe life into a fragmented world. For anyone who believes the Church still matters, this book is essential reading.

> —Rev. Lori Tapia, National Pastor and President, Obra
> Hispana of the Christian Church (Disciples of Christ)

As a regional middle judicatory leader, I am often asked by congregational leaders, "how can we thrive?" *Thriving Church* is a necessary book that helps to answer this question in an age of declining membership and declining congregations. Through vibrant narratives of diverse churches, this research affirms that thriving is not a one-size-fits-all proposition, nor is thriving about numbers. Thriving is, however, about practices that nurture the best in congregations and people. The questions at the end of the chapters makes this book a great tool for clergy and laity.

> —Rev. Dr. Donald K. Gillett, II, Regional Minister, Christian
> Church (Disciples of Christ) in Kentucky

"The Church of Jesus Christ is one of the most critical voices needed for this spectacular hour. With declining memberships, conflicted messages and mission, and a religious fatigue that threatens the survival of some of our most sacred institutions, there is good news to share. Here is a long-overdue insight shared by Cash and Wilcoxson's in their new book. It invites readers to take seriously the opportunity to thrive. This insightful book reads much like a spiritual prescription for counteracting all that threatens the vision, mission and survival of the church. I'm excited for this timely work, one which extends an invitation to the reader to move from endangerment to empowerment.

> —Rev. Dr. Christal L. Williams, Regional Minister, Christian
> Church (Disciples of Christ) in Indiana

We live in a time when being "church" causes us to feel anxious. We hear that the church is a dying institution. Why? Because it is not the way so many of us remember it. We recall when congregations had more worshipers on Sunday morning, busy Sunday Schools, robed choirs and clergy, twenty-four deacons and twelve elders. The church is different than we may remember, but it is not dying. *Thriving Congregations* tell the stories of congregations that are alive and flourishing. These congregations have found ways to respond faithfully to what God is calling them to do. They invite us to listen and learn from churches that have found a way to live in new ways and to discern the ways God is calling each of our churches to live fully into God's call.

> —Rev. Dr. LaTaunya Bynum, Regional Minister, Christian Church (Disciples of Christ) in Northern California-Nevada

Revs. Wilcoxson and Cash offer a valuable gift to the whole church—a compilation of leadership-focused wise practices drawn from living congregational examples. They combine testimony and technique, giving often-used buzzwords like *mission, vision, culture, thriving,* and *Biblical* visible hearts, heads, hands, and feet. They provide thick descriptions in place of superficial glosses, deep theological and biblical exploration, and practicable applications. This book should be used in congregational study, seminary classrooms, and veteran pastors' book circles.

> —Rev. Dr. Andy Mangum Regional Minister, Christian Church (Disciples of Christ) in the Southwest

For many church leaders, we were just grateful that our churches survived the events of 2020. But now we have an opportunity to take stock of where we find ourselves post-pandemic and ask what it might look like for our churches to thrive in the next chapter of their story. Cash and Wilcoxson offer a timely, highly practical, narrative-driven resource for churches seeking to do just that.

> —Sean Gladding, pastor and author of *The Story of God, the Story of Us*

How can churches cultivate the qualities of a thriving congregation so that they and their communities can grow? In this clear and insightful book, Erin Cash and Kory Wilcoxson share their findings from eleven compelling case studies that can be applied to nearly any congregation. *Thriving Church* is a valuable resource for the seminary classroom, congregational leaders, and ministers who are looking to take their church to the next level of flourishing.

—Rev. Dr. Leah Schade, Lexington Theological Seminary and author of *Preaching and Social Issues: Tools and Tactics for Empowering Your Prophetic Voice*

This insightful book redefines thriving congregations beyond size or budget, focusing on mission, healthy clergy, empowered laity, and meaningful success measures. It offers a refreshing, faith-filled approach that embraces unique strengths and dynamic ministry, inspiring readers to cultivate thriving, and authentic church communities rooted in purpose and the joy of the Lord! Organized around storytelling, key traits of thriving churches, and reflective questions, the format transforms reading into an active learning experience. Highly recommended!

—Rev. Dr. Denise Bell, Lexington Theological Seminary, Donald and Lillian Nunnelly Chair and Assistant Professor of Pastoral Leadership

Copyright ©2025 Erin Cash and Kory Wilcoxson

All rights reserved. For permission to reuse content, please contact Copyright Clearance Center, 222 Rosewood Drive, Danvers, MA 01923, (978) 750-8400, www.copyright.com.

Scriptures are from the *New Revised Standard Version*, Updated Edition, unless otherwise noted.

Print: 9780827237391

EPUB: 9780827237407

EPDF: 9780827237414

ChalicePress.com

"Stories make us more alive, more human, more courageous, more loving." ~ Madeline L'Engle

For the churches who tell their stories with courage and love.

Contents

Acknowledgments	xi
Introduction	xiii

Thriving Congregations...

...Are Rooted in Scripture
The Story of High Street Christian Church — 1

...Know Their Mission & Vision
The Story of South Elkhorn Christian Church — 15

...Understand Community & Rest
The Story of Daytona Beach Drive-In Christian Church — 29

...Reject a Fear Mentality
The Story of Nueva Comunidad Christian Church — 45

...Are Collaborative
The Story of Foothills Christian Church — 57

...Are Generous
The Stories of Co-Heirs with Christ and
Second Christian Church — 69

...Are Flexible
The Story of Wakonda Christian Church — 83

...Are Willing to Take Risks
The Story of Midway Christian Church — 97

...Are Forward Thinkers
The Story of New Century Fellowship Christian Church — 111

...Refuse to Be Stagnant
The Story of Beech Grove Christian Church — 123

Conclusion — 135

Acknowledgments

Thank you to Lilly Endowment, Inc. for trusting Lexington Theological Seminary to manage a grant that allowed this research to happen. This book could not have come to fruition without their generous gifts. Special thanks to Lexington Theological Seminary and Crestwood Christian Church (Disciples of Christ), who have supported us and challenged us to keep writing.

We couldn't have finished this work without the ongoing conversation and feedback from Charisse Gillett, Bruce Barkhauer, Carly Dickinson, Rosalie Calloway, Michael Swartzentruber, Brad Lyons, and our editors Ulrike Guthrie and Indu Shanmugam.

To our spouses, Chris and Amy: thank you for allowing us the time we needed to write, to talk through sections, and to travel. You are the anchors that keep us grounded in the swirling storms of life.

And finally, to the twenty-nine churches participating in the Thriving Congregations project, especially to the eleven churches featured on these pages: this is for you. Without your stories and witness, this book wouldn't exist.

Introduction

A twenty-member church in a rural town sets up tables and folding chairs in its fellowship space on a Wednesday morning and prepares a weekly community breakfast for whoever walks through the door, from the mayor to the struggling single mom. Another church, set squarely in the suburbs, faithfully stewards its endowment, offering life-changing grants to local nonprofits to help them achieve their dreams. And still another church encourages its lay leaders to give their testimony as a part of worship, modeling vulnerability and claiming the transformative power of God's Spirit, and seeks to offer bilingual services in a southwestern metropolis to reach out to more people in their city. These churches couldn't look more different, and yet each one, in its own way, is thriving.

In December 2019, Lilly Endowment, Inc. awarded a $1 million grant to Lexington Theological Seminary (LTS) to study congregations in pursuit of an answer to the question, "What makes a church thrive?" At LTS, the student's relationship with a congregation is an essential part of the educational process; the curriculum helps the student negotiate the rhythms of pastoral life and reflect upon ways clergy thrive and are challenged in their ministry context. Rooted in this understanding, the grant supported an exploration into the link between thriving congregations and student success. The Thriving Congregations Project surmised that thriving churches are anchored in four main traits: 1) a commitment to mission, 2) healthy clergy, 3) an empowered laity, and 4) a means of measuring success. Since that time, the research of the Thriving Congregations Project has shown that these are indeed critical pathways for a church to follow if it wants to thrive.

However, LTS also learned that thriving churches have other qualities in common. The attributes featured in this book are the result of that research. While these are not the only traits thriving churches possess, these are the traits that we feel are relevant to the broadest swath of congregations. These are the traits that we believe will help your congregation thrive, too.

Defining Thriving

Thriving is one of those words that is difficult to nail down. While a textbook definition may be elusive, you typically know a thriving congregation when you see one. For us and for the work of LTS, thriving is about a congregation's ability to embrace its identity fully and faithfully, still allowing for adaption and resilience as culture shifts and challenges arise. Thriving is not always about membership size, the number of visitors coming through the doors, the type of building you have (or do not have), or the bottom line on the budget sheet. Congregations at any stage in their life cycle can be thriving churches.

Thriving is about living into who God is calling your church to be at this time and in this place. The traits this book presents are characteristics of thriving churches; they are not prerequisites that classify you as a thriving church. Thriving churches, particularly the churches in LTS's project, exhibit these traits to different degrees. Some of them excel at one particular trait, yet clearly have room for growth in others. While a few churches are living out several of these traits well, no churches excel at all of them. Thriving does not have to mean you have all of these traits at the same time and with the same level of giftedness. Being a thriving church is a journey, not a destination.

Consider thriving as a Venn diagram with each of the traits being one circle. Some churches will be excellent at one or two traits, while others may excel at four or five. The "thriving-est" churches (yes, we made up that word!) are the ones closest to the center of the diagram, where all of the circles overlap; they are actively seeking to embody as many of the traits as possible. The goal is not to place yourself on the diagram and simply accept that as the way it has to be. It's a starting point from where you can continue to move toward the center. From here, thriving churches find new ways to live into as many traits as possible, or to live as deeply as possible into one trait, in their specific context.

The Stories We Tell

The Thriving Congregations Project has partnered with twenty-nine congregations since 2019. In addition, hundreds of congregations participated in *Thriving Together*, a workshop series the project hosted. We chose to tell the stories of these particular eleven churches for two reasons.

First, we wanted to reflect the diversity of setting, ethnicity, congregational size, age, and clergy staff that went into our choice of the churches that participated in the project. As LTS leaders put together the first cohort, they paid particular attention to making sure it represented a diverse spectrum of congregations. The grant tasked LTS with partnering with four Regions of the Christian Church (Disciples of Christ): Kentucky, Florida, Arizona, and the Upper Midwest (which encompasses Iowa, Minnesota, and North and South Dakota). Project leaders invited congregations to participate based on a recommendation from their Regional Minister at the time and their current connection to LTS. For the sake of the project, LTS wanted to begin with congregations about which they already knew a little. The participating churches in the first cohort were 50 percent Caucasian, 18 percent African American, and 14 percent Latinx; they were 64 percent urban/suburban congregations and 14 percent rural congregations. Large churches (those over 150 members) made up 41 percent of the project, and churches of fewer than 75 members made up 23 percent of the project. In total, 27 percent of the churches in the first cohort had bivocational pastors. If you did the math, you would notice that these percentages do not add up to 100. Several churches in the project fall somewhere else in the category; a few churches are "intentionally multiethnic," or "small town" churches, for example.

In 2023, LTS was able to convene a second cohort of congregations which consisted of seven African American congregations in Kentucky. Of those churches, three had bivocational pastors. All but one of the congregations are urban/suburban congregations. They range in size from 40 to approximately 200 members. Two of these congregations appear in the following chapters.

Second, we chose these particular churches because we wanted you to see your congregation in at least one chapter. We hope that you can relate to the story of one church (or more!). Maybe your congregation is small and just beginning, like Nueva Comunidad in Winter Park, Florida. Or maybe you participate in an historic congregation like High Street Christian Church in Mt. Sterling, Kentucky. It may be that your church is predominantly an aging congregation, like Midway Christian Church in Midway, Kentucky. Or maybe your church has a lot of young families, like Foothills Christian Church in Phoenix, Arizona. Whatever church looks like to you, we hope you can see yourself in some of the stories that follow.

Third and finally, in some ways the churches' stories chose themselves. When we sat down to consider the question, "Which churches' stories do we want to tell?" we were flooded with ideas. Every church that participated in the Thriving Congregations Project had a story to tell. Churches like Crestwood Christian Church in Lexington, Kentucky, where Kory pastors, also have remarkable stories about the way they live into these traits. We chose to share the stories of churches you might otherwise not hear. As we thought about the many stories we could tell, the ones we ultimately chose are the ones that are the most unique (like a church in an old drive-in movie theater) and yet also relatable (like the challenge of building community in our fractured and fast-paced world). We hope they inspire you to think differently about how you might live out these traits of thriving church. About two-thirds of all Disciples of Christ congregations worship with fewer than fifty persons on a Sunday morning, and the denomination has around 250 new church starts (around 8 percent of the denomination); we wanted to make sure those churches were highlighted!

Denominational Similarity

The parameters set by the 2019 grant from Lilly Endowment, Inc. meant that LTS would work with congregations which partner closely with LTS and which their Regional Minister could recommend. Thus, all of the first cohort of twenty-two churches were from the Christian Church (Disciples of Christ) tradition.

Introduction xvii

The second cohort broadened denominational representation and shortened the cohort timeline. As LTS looked for ways it might continue the work through a Sustainability or Scaling Grant from Lilly Endowment, Inc. it sought to broaden our reach with congregations which had a relationship with LTS, but whose commonality was different. Since the first cohort had all been Disciples of Christ congregations, LTS next tried a different commonality: members of the second cohort were all African American churches in Kentucky, but not all of them were Disciples of Christ. Instead, the second cohort of seven had four Disciples of Christ congregations, two Baptist congregations, and one African Methodist Episcopal congregation. The objective in the second cohort was to learn how denominational differences added to our understanding of thriving.

While we know that the stories of the non-Disciples churches are equally vibrant and also exhibit the traits of thriving congregations, for the sake of continuity here we choose to tell only stories from within the Disciples of Christ denomination. That being said, we also know intuitively that church is church regardless of the name on its sign. We believe that most (if not all) churches seek to follow God's call, strive to be generous, and endeavor to be faithful in taking risks or working collaboratively. So we've sought to write these chapters in a way that doesn't highlight denominational particularities but instead captures the essence of being Christ's body in this world. These traits are woven through churches of all flavors and names.

What we learned from our second cohort is that the traits found in this book do cross denominational lines. Both Baptist churches and the AME church found the project to be meaningful to their work. Likewise, we hope that even if your church is not a member of the Christian Church (Disciples of Christ), you will see yourself in these pages.

About the Authors

We believe it is always helpful to know something about the authors of a book, particularly when those authors are new to the publishing world. We have chosen to tell you about who we are in a way that models for you what we hope you learn from this book: This book is an exercise in seeing the unique ways your congregation is already thriving and how you can further develop your thriving traits. Sometimes it is difficult to see those traits in your own church. Therefore, you need to take a step back and try to see the church as if you're someone from the outside. In that spirit, we have written these paragraphs for one another; Kory wrote the paragraphs about Erin and Erin wrote the paragraphs about Kory.

Kory is the Senior Pastor at Crestwood Christian Church in Lexington, Kentucky, just a few miles from the LTS offices. Crestwood was one of the first churches to say yes to participating in the initial cohort of the Thriving Congregations Project. Crestwood is a congregation with a history of long-tenured pastors. And Kory is continuing that trend; he celebrated his fifteenth anniversary there in November 2024. Kory's leadership at Crestwood has enabled the congregation to take some critical steps in reorganizing their staff, seeing their giftedness in new ways, and strengthening their partnerships both with the ministries in Lexington and with the other Disciples of Christ congregations in that city.

Kory is a natural and gifted storyteller. He holds two degrees in Communication (a B.A. from Indiana University and an M.A. from Ohio University), and two degrees in Religion (an M.Div. from Christian Theological Seminary in Indianapolis, Indiana, and a D.Min. from Lexington Theological Seminary in Lexington, Kentucky). In another life before ministry he worked as a journalist. He is curious and energetic in his research and writing. Kory did the congregational interviews for these chapters, and in a few settings I (Erin) was his designated notetaker. He would become so excited by the stories these churches were telling that I would have to ask him to slow down so that I could get all of the notes recorded!

Professional qualifications aside, Kory was the obvious choice as a coauthor because of Crestwood's long partnership with LTS. Crestwood has faithfully and lovingly supported LTS in its best and brightest days and in its most difficult. The Crestwood congregation has given of their financial gifts, their space (LTS graduations have been held at Crestwood for years), and their people to help LTS be the best version of itself. Pastors and lay leaders at Crestwood have served on the LTS Board of Trustees; students have come through our doors and walked across the graduation stage; and seminary employees have been faithful members of Crestwood. When searching for a co-author, how could I not begin that search at Crestwood?

Kory is a husband, a father to two grown daughters, an avid hiker, a trusted friend to many, a dog parent, and an Enneagram 3. Whatever he sets out to do, he does with excellence.

I have had the privilege of knowing **Erin** for many years as a colleague, writing partner, and friend. When we first met, she was fairly new to the Disciples world, having made the jump from the Cooperative Baptist Fellowship along with her husband, Chris. Erin was serving as Minister to Children at First Christian Church in Paducah, Kentucky when she was called to be the Director of Admissions at LTS.

After nine years in that position (during which she also recruited me to start my D.Min.!) she transitioned to her current role as Project Director of the Thriving Congregations Project. For the last five years, Erin has worked tirelessly to connect congregations to each other for the purpose of learning how we can support each other in our quest to be thriving congregations. Erin's exemplary organization, clear and constant communication, and boundless encouragement have helped the congregations in the project live into their call to thrive.

For this book, Erin has written the observational/lessons learned portions. She's been able to take a balcony view of the twenty-nine churches in the Thriving Congregations Project and has keenly observed the common traits that have emerged in that work. Her ability to distill five years of research and relationships into these ten chapters is a testament to her ability to gather data, find points of overlap, and synthesize raw material into information that is easy to understand and immensely helpful to those on the receiving end of her wisdom.

Erin holds a B.A. in Religion/Philosophy and English from Greenville College (now Greenville University) in Greenville, Illinois;

an M.Div. from Candler School of Theology at Emory University; and a D.Min. from Lexington Theological Seminary. Erin and I enrolled in the same D.Min. cohort at LTS, and the group of nine of which we were a part embarked on a "fun-filled" journey of coursework, online discussions, a few pages of reading, and, ultimately, a final project. I was only able to cross the finish line with Erin's support.

Erin and her husband, Chris, are avid travelers, usually seeking out a baseball stadium, a national park, or a scenic hike. Once, my wife and I even met up with them at a Colorado Rockies game while on vacation out West! She is a bonus mom to Ella, dog mom to Ivy, and active member of First Christian Church in Georgetown, Kentucky. It's been a true joy to tell these stories with her.

How to Use this Book

As we've said, our hope is that everyone who reads this book will see themselves and their church in at least one chapter, both in the identity of the church and in the trait it exemplifies. Of course, that also means that there will be several chapters in which you won't see yourself. But we do hope you hear faint notes of your congregation's melody, even if you don't yet personally know the words to the song. It could be that reading about a church context different than your own may spark your imagination to see and act beyond the familiar.

Our goal is for this book to be not only informational but practical. We don't want you only to read it, but also to use it. Each chapter ends with some scripture references and discussion questions to help you reflect on the trait described in that chapter. We hope this will be helpful for ministerial staff, church boards, elder's groups, and Sunday school classes as they discern and dream about their congregation's future. We also envisage this book being useful to denominational executives who want to help congregations map a path forward for strategic planning. The book doesn't have to be read beginning to end. Each chapter stands alone, so you can jump right into any chapter that you think will be helpful to you.

Thriving Congregations Are Rooted in Scripture

The Story of High Street Christian Church, Mt. Sterling, Kentucky

Pastor Darrell Hayden tells the story of an elder in his church who loves to bellow out the opening lines of Psalm 107 when he's in front of the congregation on Sunday morning at High Street Christian Church in Mt. Sterling, Kentucky. "Give thanks to the Lord for he is good!" the elder shouts. "His steadfast love endures forever!" In summer, if they open the doors of the sanctuary, people up and down High Street can hear this elder shouting scripture from the top of his lungs.

Darrell tells how one time a white congregation was worshipping with his primarily African American congregation and this particular elder was serving at the table. Darrell was expecting this elder to blow the roof off the place with his holy holler, but instead he spoke the words timidly, more like a church mouse than a mouthpiece of God. When the elder finished, Darrell said he looked at him and said, "Now, say it right." "What?" asked the elder. "Say it right. Don't tone it down," replied Darrell.

There's nothing toned down about the way in which High Street Christian Church proclaims the word of God to the folks of Mt. Sterling, a small town a forty-five minute drive east of Lexington. In fact, in 2024, High Street celebrated 150 years of preaching the good news. "You don't get to be a 150-year-old church if you're not rooted in scripture," says church member, Gene Caston. "The seeds that were planted by Preston Taylor (the founder of the church) is what we see right now. Over time, the roots have expanded themselves and

2 THRIVING CHURCH

deepened." Those seeds continue to bear fruit as they are watered and nurtured by Darrell and the leaders of High Street.

As we sit in High Street's sanctuary, the space is all decked out for Christmas, with garlands and Christmas trees and an Advent candle. That seemed to be the appropriate season to talk about how the Bible is a living document for this congregation. Its people not only worship Emmanuel, "God with us," but they live out that ethos by taking God's word and putting it into action in their lives.

"I hope (scripture) conveys that a person wants to reflect on what's coming next in their lives," says Darrell, who's been at High Street for twenty-nine years. "The scripture should reveal to us that, no matter what we're getting ready to face this week, we have the word of God with us." Darrell says he lets the Holy Spirit guide him on what to preach each Sunday, trusting that the Spirit will lead him to the "right word" that his congregation needs to hear that day. "We have to love in the places where the scripture falls. It might smack me today, but I still gotta be loved. When you've been cut with the sword of the Spirit, you still need to be loved. I think that's really what the scripture is calling out to do."

That call leaves an impression on his congregation that lingers well beyond the worship service. "When Pastor Hayden preaches, he uses multiple scriptures to tie the sermon together," says Gene. "You take what he preaches and bring it into ourselves and apply it to our daily lives." Scripture not only informs the sermon, but also the hymns, prayers, and other aspects of worship at High Street. "When we're in worship, there's a presence of the Holy Spirit—it's in the air," said Gene.

Gene's wife, Wanda, echoes those sentiments about Darrell's sermons. "His preaching, it starts up there with him," she says, "but then it flows out and if you're paying attention, it sits with you for a minute. As you're looking at the scripture, it comes more alive and you want to see it again."

A congregation that roots itself in scripture recognizes that God's word not only provides spiritual grounding, but also has a relevant word to speak, compelling a response. In a sense, the Bible is not just static words on the page, but alive and living. Darrell not only preaches this, but lives it out, even when no one is listening.

For example, one year High Street participated in a community New Year's Eve watch night service. The service featured three straight hours of scripture reading. Darrell says someone asked him why he kept reading the scriptures out loud when no one was there to hear them. Darrell explained that, "The scripture was so present it felt like it was in the atmosphere. It doesn't matter if you're listening directly because the Spirit is there." Not only is all scripture God-breathed, as Paul says, but it is also the spiritual oxygen we take in that inspires us and enables us to live out our faith.

That carries real significance for Darrell's congregation as they let God's word and their connection at High Street minister to them. Brandi Taul, a church member who has experienced significant health issues, says while in a nursing home, "I can look to my left and look to my right and see that it's worse for others than it is for me." Brandi remarks about a recent trip out west and how she was overwhelmed by God's handiwork, a memory which sustains her in her current condition. "That's how I know we're rooted in scripture," says Gene. "She can be stuck in bed and still have such a strong faith."

The faith formation at High Street is pervasive in the congregation, thanks to Darrell's willingness to present the Bible as it is. "He doesn't try to sugar coat it or run and hide from the hard themes," Wanda said. Faith is often forged in the midst of difficulty and challenges as we let the Spirit connect our story with God's story. "I had a member talk about Jesus' broken body," says Darrell, "and a woman went all to pieces over that. She trembled like the world was coming to an end. It's hard to hear. But the scripture should move us like that!"

It does move us—and in ways more powerful than we could ever orchestrate on our own. Gene had a family member in Minnesota who was murdered, and Gene was asked to speak at the funeral on the spur of the moment. The message he shared was about "making something good happen" in the midst of tragedy, which was exactly

4 THRIVING CHURCH

the word Darrell had preached the Sunday before. "He preached it, it resonated with me, and I could share it with our family 850 miles away," says Gene. That family has since joined the church, Darrell has baptized them, and they tune in every Sunday to hear God's word on the church's livestream.

That's the beauty and the challenge of preaching. Anyone who's stood in a pulpit knows that when we endeavor to share the good news, we never know who is really listening, either in person or online. Sometimes the people we deem least likely to pay attention are the ones in whom the word is taking root. "In the early 2000s, we had a group of our kids doing T-shirts," says Darrell. "We were trying to come up with a theme. One of the kids says, 'Let's do Top 10 Sermons.'" Darrell replies that he was sure they couldn't name even one of his sermons, let alone ten—and instead they named fifteen! "It blew me away that they were listening that much," he says. "You're depositing into people something treasured and they're listening. That's what the word is supposed to do."

And, at High Street, it does. As with the Elder's boisterous broadcasting of scripture, the proclamation of God's word starts in the building but then emanates out into the world in ways that make God's kin-dom known. Gene says, "We try to encourage fellowship among our members and other churches and social organizations through our work in the community." That means being cognizant of the responsibility they carry. "Our leaders...really try to model being Christ-like in the things we do, to be good representatives of Christ and not just the church," says Gene. "What happens here through the scriptures should make us do what's right in the world," Darrell adds.

When a congregation listens to God's word as intently as High Street Church does, putting it into action is such a natural next step that it doesn't require a committee to make decisions. Darrell talks about one particular family in the community for which the church was helping to carry a burden. "A couple started helping with the family as they fell apart. Some started picking up the pieces, and the church followed suit." There was no meeting to decide to do this; people just naturally responded to the need. "To me, that's what's scripture is all about," Darrell says. "People just came in and did what we had to do. I think it's unique to see people just step up and see the scriptures lived out like that."

What helps in this ongoing mission to put God's word into action is High Street's clarity about who they are and who God has called them to be, and how that identity is firmly grounded in the Bible. In the last few years, using Habakkuk 2:2 as a guide, the congregation finalized their mission statement: "A Now Generation People of faith, refreshing, uniting, and serving our community, while searching [for], praising, and worshipping the Kingdom of God." Gene says, "The Lord told me, 'These are the scriptures that go with that mission statement.' It was affirming to me that we had rooted ourselves in scripture without really even being actively aware of it." A video Gene put together shows the various ways in which High Street is living out its mission and, along with pictures from Vacation Bible School and a fellowship picnic, it contains no fewer than eight scripture references

That's not surprising considering Darrell's commitment to saturating his people with God's word. His sermons function as an anointing, as each Sunday he pours out God's word like oil, letting it seep into his congregation. He's been doing this for almost thirty years and yet he still has a relevant word to speak each Sunday. There have been times when God has given him a specific word to preach to a particular person, and Darrell has obediently followed, permeating his sermon with scripture references that are as timely as the day's headlines. "A week or two after Donald Trump got elected [president in 2024]," says Darrell, "I preached Psalm 24. It talks about the priest going around hollering, 'Who is the King of Glory?' and the people were yelling, 'The Lord!'"

Darrell isn't afraid to tackle tough issues because he knows that in the end the sermon's not about him. It's about what God is doing through God's word to bring healing, wholeness, and unity. And the place in which that is made most manifest for Darrell and the High Street congregation is at the center of their worship space. "It's the table," says Darrell. Notice Darrell doesn't call it "our" table, because he knows High Street is called to be stewards of a much greater mystery represented by the bread and the cup. High Street doesn't own the table: the people are simply the ones who do the inviting, following Jesus' lead. "Everyone is welcome," says Darrell. "We can find reassurance and peace and joy at the tale, and everyone has always been welcomed there. That has been our center."

Darrell recognizes that the word of God represented by the communion table speaks so much louder than anything he or the other leaders of High Street could express. "The table is our center point, past the preaching, past the worship. In the African American church, it represents that the broken, the downtrodden are welcome." Through slavery, through Jim Crow, through modern-day divisions, the table has stayed constant. "You'd go to the lunch counters and you weren't welcome, but at this table, that wasn't the case. The table symbolizes all of that history for us."

For this congregation, turning 150 means continuing to honor that history while also being nimble enough to let God's word dictate the path forward into the future, a future embodied by one of the youngest members. "Jeremiah—he's nine—can't wait to get to Sunday School, to bless the offering, to sing, to usher, to offer a prayer," Gene said. In reference to former youth who have moved on from Mt. Sterling, Darrell says, "They're watching on Facebook. We're meeting them in a different way. They want to be connected to the church. Because they're listening."

When the Thriving Congregations Project at LTS began working together on what it means to be rooted in scripture, the congregations were divided. Some of the church members—particularly the pastors—were concerned about how the phrase might offend those who were recovering from church trauma. Scripture has often been used to support abusive relationships, misogyny, homophobia, and many other traumas, "The Bible says ..." has been the beginning of more than one hurtful and even traumatizing justification. Other congregations, however, recognized the centrality of scripture for the work we do. For if the church isn't rooted in scripture, does it have any roots at all?

So how does a thriving church balance the challenges of using the scripture to ground its work? For congregations like High Street, scriptures are at the heart of everything they do—worship, prayer, fellowship, studies, relationships within their families and among one another. The laity are just as familiar with the words of the Bible as the leaders. They read it, memorize it, study it, pray it, and quote it daily. They live out Deuteronomy 6:4–9, carving the scriptures not just into their worship services and promotional videos, but into their hearts and lives.

Being immersed in scripture means you can't pick and choose to which parts you pay attention. You can't excise from the Bible the passages that are troublesome or have been misused down through history. It is true that scripture has long been used to repress and oppress people in harmful ways. And yet it is also true that it can be redeemed. Naming the ways in which the Bible has been used to damage rather than give life enables the text to be reimagined in the ears of those it has wounded.

Erin can testify to this personally. She was born as a Southern Baptist in the days before inerrancy and fundamentalism took over the denomination. As she grew and as the denomination changed, the Bible became more and more of a weapon used against her and against anyone who didn't think like those inside the church. She studied the scriptures vigorously as a youth and young adult, searching for a deeper relationship with God, wrestling with her sense of call, and struggling to find her place in a denomination which told her that God would never call her to anything other than being a missionary or a pastor's wife. So when she began to pull away from the denomination of her ancestors, she also pulled away from the Bible. The answers were in books *about* the Bible, not the Bible itself. The Bible was a source of pain, but as she read book after book explaining what the Bible actually meant, her wounds healed over and became scars, and she was able to return to the Bible as a source of comfort, teaching, and learning. But the hesitance to hold the scripture in such high regard remained; after all, if it could do that much damage to a cis-hetero white person, how much more could it harm and ostracize already marginalized people?

8   THRIVING CHURCH

Often, moderate and progressive churches fear reclaiming the Bible. These congregations become safe havens for denominational refugees from other places that have wounded them. In their effort to remain sensitive to the pain and trauma that many believers and former believers carry, they handle the scripture lightly, embracing it only gingerly. Sunday School and small groups do book studies about theological principles (grace, justice, love, prayer, etc.) but often do not study the text itself. In so doing, they have developed a generation of faithful disciples who understand deep theological concepts but have very little scriptural literacy. Like the seed scattered on rocky ground, their faith withers when the sun becomes too hot, and their scriptural roots cannot draw enough nourishment for the journey. Churches like High Street that are deeply rooted in scripture find a balance between not taking scripture literally and not taking it seriously enough.

Literally Understood

Let us be clear: we are not advocating that the scripture be understood literally. If we believe that the Word of God is living and active, we must also believe that the scripture speaks differently to different people, based on language, culture, context, timing, identity, and countless other traits. How often have you read a familiar passage and found an entirely new meaning than you've ever considered before? That's the living Word of God at work, and it deserves to be honored. That oft-cited verse, 2 Timothy 3:16, says "All scripture is God-breathed" (NIV), not "All scripture is God dictated word for word." In fact, to read the Bible in a modern language is to read it at least two translations (sometimes more) away from the original languages of the authors. The ancient texts from which translators do their work have been passed down for generations. We do not have an original manuscript handwritten by Paul; we have copies and adjustments, commentaries and memories.

To say that you are rooted in scripture is not to say that the text speaks literally. Instead, it is to say that the source of our vision, our values, our studies, and our lives should be found in the scriptures. Like High Street, we should be reading it regularly, absorbing it, pondering it, and inviting it to shape our stories of who God is calling us to be right now and right where we are. The scripture should hang in the very air we breathe.

Scripturally Rooted

Consider the roots of a plant. Plants rely on three elements to sustain their life: sunshine, water, and soil. Two of those three nutrients derive from the roots. Houseplants need to be repotted approximately every year because the soil runs out of nutrients. The roots draw up water and nutrients into the whole being of the plant, encouraging growth, allowing flowers to bloom, and adding strength to the structure.

The roots also provide stability. If, in the process of a plant being repotted, too many of the roots are damaged, the plant is too weak to support itself. It leans to the side, or it flops over at the leaves. A plant without roots in the soil is too weak to thrive.

The same is true of the church which does not root itself in scripture. Only listening to the text quoted before the sermon or at the communion table is insufficient to build up the whole body: it provides just enough sustenance for life, but not enough for thriving. Our roots must dig deep into the scriptures to find what we need to flourish.

Congregations deepen their roots in the scripture by study. Small groups, Bible studies, prayer groups that practice *lectio divina* and other methods of listening to the scriptures are some of the ways churches grow their roots. They center their worship experience in the text and do not just relegate it to one reading each week. They begin board meetings with a scripture; their elders begin meetings with a meditation on a text. The scriptures shape the vision and mission of the congregation. Children learn how to use their Bibles and pray aloud.

For some pastors and lay leaders, finding good source material from which to study is challenging. As many progressive and mainline churches shut their publishing operations, available curriculum is increasingly conservative. We recommend talking with the faith leaders of your denomination to locate curricula that fit the theological

10 THRIVING CHURCH

positions of your congregation and focus heavily on the scriptures. If no such material comes to the surface, there are many commentary series that are accessible to lay leaders; with their help, you can foster a robust conversation about the text. Two such examples are the *New Testament for Everyone* series by Tom (N.T.) Wright, from (the Anglican or Episcopalian) SPCK Publishing, and *Interpretation* published by (the Presbyterian) Westminster John Knox Press. Regardless of the resources you use, the goal is to keep the discussion rooted in the scriptural text and not in the commentary.

By Their Fruits

Plants that grow deep roots bear fruit. They flower. They share their nutrients with humans, animals, and insects as they take what they have absorbed and give it away as food for another. The fruits that grow from thriving plants contribute to their ecosystem and, in turn, are supported by that very same system.

Like High Street, the flourishing church that is rooted in scripture has the capacity to share its growth with those around it. The text becomes embodied and shared as we draw up more nutrition from the Word of God. Being rooted in scripture is not simply for the sake of having a deeper relationship with God, individually or collectively: it's for the world. When the living, breathing scriptures indwell the congregation, fruit begins to grow. Psalm 1 says those who study the scriptures are "like trees planted by streams of water, which yield their fruit in its season, and their leaves do not wither" (1:3).

Study of the scriptures allows us to be knowledgeable about the text, which is one of the few things we all have in common across the life of the church. "If we agree that it's authoritative (not literal, but authoritative) and a common basis for our discernment, then we are strengthened when we are able to engage with the text individually and corporately," says Disciples of Christ General Minister and President, Terri Hord Owens. "The whole body is strengthened when we all have familiarity and knowledge of our common foundation." We cannot grow good fruits if we are spiritually dry, and our leaves are withered away.

Preaching the Gospel

How often have pastors had to preach on particularly divisive topics? How often have they wrestled with a text, struggling to find the right words to say to a divided congregation? In one particularly hostile election season, Kory told his congregation, "I'm going to hide behind Jesus these next few weeks. What you're hearing are the words of Jesus, not me." He didn't use this as an excuse, but as a way to remind the congregation that Jesus's words are sometimes difficult to hear. Sometimes Jesus says things we do not like or that challenge a particular belief we hold.

Preaching the Gospel means honoring the difficulties in the scriptures and reminding the people in the pews that the English translation of the Bible is not always gentle and friendly; some of the texts are hard, and wrestling with them is beneficial. Preaching is one of the ways in which pastors can help their congregations root themselves deeper in the Bible. The preacher who continues to return to the text is modeling the struggle for the congregation. Witnessing the preacher admit, "This text is challenging to me; at first reading, I struggle with what the text says here," invites the laity to see the nuances of scripture lived out in front of them. It encourages them to dig deeper into the soil of their faith and find places where their faith can take root.

Biblical literacy promoted from the pulpit and in faith formation circles helps people connect the dots between their values, the Bible, and their faith. One pastor in the Thriving Congregations Project says of her congregation's history, "We have so many people who have come from different traditions. They don't understand why the scripture calls us to love the poor and marginalized; for example, they know they're supposed to care for the poor, but they don't know *why*."

A Relevant Word

Congregations rooted in scripture do not have to be relegated to literal readings and extreme fundamentalism. Moderate and progressive congregations need to reclaim their heritage as "People of

12 THRIVING CHURCH

the Book." If we do not know the texts that shape our narrative, how will we ever be faithful disciples? Without writing the scriptures on our hearts we cannot live them out. Even the congregation which roots itself in justice, kindness, acceptance, or other biblical traits misses the opportunity to understand *why* we are a congregation committed to such traits if it does not connect them to the biblical stories. Our work bears more fruit when we understand the origins of what we believe.

> *Our world defines "thriving" in a number of different ways, and it is then eager to sell us the latest tools and tricks to live out that definition. But God's people know there's only one book they need in order to thrive and it's the one we've been following for centuries. The Judeo-Christian tradition has as its foundation the primary revelation of God given to us through scripture. And within that book are several examples of the blessings of following God's world.*
>
> *In Luke 6, Jesus tells the story of the two builders, one who built his house on the sand and the other who built his on rock. The one whose house is built on rock and withstands the floods of life is the one who hears Jesus' words and lives them out. The psalmist highlights the illuminating role of scripture when he writes, "Your word is a lamp to my feet and a light to my path" (Ps. 119:105). And Paul reminds Timothy to keep the Bible central to his ministry when Paul writes, "All scripture is inspired by God and is useful for teaching, for reproof, for correction, and for training in righteousness..." (2 Tim. 3:16).*

Texts for Study

- Psalm 1
- Deuteronomy 6:4–9
- Matthew 13:18–23
- I Peter 3:13–16
- Romans 10:5–17
- I Corinthians 3:9–11
- Luke 6:46–49

QUESTIONS FOR DISCUSSION AND REFLECTION

1. What does *being rooted in scripture* look like for your congregation? What can you put into practice from Deuteronomy 6: 4–9 that will help your congregation grow deeper roots?

2. What biblical principles are at the core of your mission and values? What scriptures support your priorities?

3. How can your church reframe its values to incorporate the scriptures? For example, if your church's mission is to care for the marginalized in your community, how might you modify the language in your statement to incorporate the texts you named in response to question 2?

4. Which of the scriptures listed above speaks to you the most? Why? What can you take away from reading them that will change your study of the Bible?

5. What are your congregation's biggest challenges with studying the Bible?

Thriving Congregations Know Their Mission and Vision

The Story of South Elkhorn Christian Church, Lexington, Kentucky

Perhaps the single most pervasive trait of any congregation seeking to be a thriving church is a clear understanding of its mission and vision. Without a sense of who the congregation is striving to be, the other traits lose their grounding in God's unique call to this particular body of Christ. A church can take risks, for example, but without a sense of where God is leading, it will continue to try new things without a sense of purpose. Knowing who you are is a prerequisite to knowing where you are going.

One church in the Thriving Congregations Initiative exemplifies this trait. South Elkhorn Christian Church (Disciples of Christ) in Lexington, Kentucky embodies the need for a church to embrace its past in a way that informs rather than impeding its future while seeking to respond to God's call. South Elkhorn has the impressive claim of being one of the oldest continuously worshiping congregations in Kentucky. It established its roots in Upper Spotsylvania, Virginia in 1767, and then moved westward through the Cumberland Gap, before setting up on the banks of South Elkhorn Creek in 1783.

The current location of the church is prime real estate for a thriving congregation seeking to expand its presence and influence. Situated on the outskirts of Lexington, South Elkhorn is in one of the fastest growing areas of the city. In 2017, the church sold some of its property for development, and now is situated within walking distance of several restaurants, coffee shops, and housing developments. This once rural church is now solidly suburban.

Rev. Michael Swartzentruber came to South Elkhorn in 2015, one of the youngest senior pastors in the church's existence. In some ways, calling him was a bold move for a congregation so steeped in its history. Michael says, "The church was looking to invest in the future, especially as there had been momentum with the growth of children and youth ministry," thanks to the excellent work of associate minister Rev. Holly Fuqua. This was Michael's first call as senior pastor, and he was eager to apply his learning and experience to a church with so much potential. Michael was ready for South Elkhorn. But was the congregation ready for the mission-focused style of leadership he was bringing?

Most pastors take at least a year or so to learn the ethos of a church before beginning to suggest changes and lead the congregation toward a new vision. Michael didn't have that luxury, thanks to an impactful decision in July 2015. The Supreme Court ruled on the legality of same-sex marriage, and immediately an LGBTQIA+ member of South Elkhorn wanted to get married. Michael's leadership was tested right away on a potentially divisive issue.

South Elkhorn stepped into a discernment process for the remainder of the year, culminating in a congregational vote that clarified that ministers can perform weddings for anyone on the church campus (including same-sex couples). The process set the tone for Michael's leadership at South Elkhorn. He says, "While some people left the church, that moment was crucial for developing a healthier congregational culture, clarity on welcome, and energy for the future." The church was able to weather the storm of division and departures, and the whole experience created confidence in Michael's ability to lead the congregation through future turbulence.

While Michael may not have wanted to deal with such conflict so early in his ministry at South Elkhorn, how the church engaged that conflict prepared the soil for the deeper, more foundational work at hand: helping South Elkhorn craft a vision and mission that would guide the church in its future service to God's kin-dom. The church already had a mission statement in place when Michael arrived, but it was fairly basic and didn't speak to the uniqueness of South Elkhorn's existence. In addition, a sign in front of the church offered the generic, almost self-contradictory label, "A seriously friendly church." Michael had just gone through the integration of a new mission/values branding process at his previous church, where he had served as youth minister, so he had first-hand experience of how a well-done process could provide clarity for the congregation, create connections through the process, and enable the senior minister to articulate a direction for the church's ministry and energize the congregation to pursue it.

Michael convened a Vision Team to study the book *Church Unique* by Will Mancini, which his previous church had also used for its process. Michael said he found the book compelling because "it took what we already had at South Elkhorn (the call to love God and others) and showed why we needed to go further, to clarify the unique way the congregation does that."

As Michael settled into South Elkhorn, he began to understand the congregation more deeply. For example, while he did indeed find the congregation to be "friendly," he knew that that label was not very distinctive or inspiring, and that the church needed more compelling and particular language to bring its values into focus. He also found that some aspects of the church's life didn't line up well with its governing structure. As Michael and South Elkhorn continued to grow together, his dreams grew bigger, bolder, and more robust. Vision Team member, Scott Brown says, "His ability to see what we could be or become was the driving force for the process."

That doesn't mean the process went quickly. Michael and the Vision Team wanted to make sure all voices were heard during the process, which not only slowed things down, but also sometimes muddied the water on the direction in which God was calling them. Still, the team persevered, and in 2021, four years and a pandemic after it was launched in 2017, the process culminated with the unveiling of a new mission and church branding. While you might assume that the pace frustrated the new senior pastor who was eager to implement his ideas, Michael says, "The long-stew was actually great. It takes time for creative ideas to emerge."

Those ideas built upon the church's history while pointing the congregation in exciting new directions. For example, the idea of the

18 THRIVING CHURCH

church being "seriously friendly" became the value of "extravagant welcome" and led to meaningful conversations about what this value meant and why it mattered to so many people. This not only provided focus for the congregation's future direction; it also helped further the healing coming out of the same-sex marriage decision.

In addition, part of the branding process was a new logo, which featured a series of asymmetrical wavy lines, that pays homage to the church's creek-connected past, evokes images of water stirred up at a baptism, and symbolizes the fluidity of the Spirit's ongoing call to the congregation. The church's future was crystallizing through Michael's leadership and the Vision Team's dedication to helping the church chart a path forward.

The thoughtful implementation of the Vision Team's results matched the deliberateness of the initial process. The Vision Team started with a soft launch of the identifying statements, which meant no one in the congregation was surprised when they were officially adopted. Michael was intentional about using some of the previous language (e.g., "a family of faith") during his first few years at South Elkhorn. By doing so, he was able to connect the church's previous understanding of itself to this new process, creating continuity between who it had been and who God was calling it to be.

One of the reasons the new vision and mission were so well received is that most of what the congregation learned about itself throughout the process wasn't new. Instead, the process reverberated with concepts the congregation already intuitively knew but didn't yet have the vocabulary to articulate. That is part of what led to the congregation's positive reception of the final product. Michael notes, "When it was 'rolled out,' it wasn't new. It had been 'dripped' into the language of the church for years, so in some ways, it was met with, 'Well, yeah....'"

Many churches spend significant time, resources, and energy on this process of defining and articulating their mission, and yet when they come to an end, they are both so glad to be finished and so exhausted from the work that the fruits of their labors are placed on a shelf to be viewed but never tasted. South Elkhorn was committed not only to doing the work but also to living out the results. The new branding took effect right away, with changes made to the bulletin, website, and all printed materials, right down to a new color palette. The story of South Elkhorn was being told in a vibrant, eye-catching new way.

Michael notes that this kind of work is "never done"—but this is precisely what he finds compelling about the model the church used. For example, he notes, "We are considering reworking one of the values because it's not currently resonating (with the congregation) and there seems to be something missing in the list of values meant to fuel everything we do together as church." Michael says that value may be lacking in both description and aspiration, and the model allows for this kind of constant evaluation and adjustment to match the changing nature of the church. Michael continues, "So we are discerning a sustainable process for strategic planning that flows *from* our mission/values and is responsive to the needs of the community."

The results of the process are now three years old, so Michael is already leading the congregation in thinking about next steps. He is working with church leaders on a strategic planning process that will use the values to inform ministry planning. He says, "In the next year and beyond, how will we be more 'extravagantly welcoming'? What 'courageous conversations' do we need to have as church?" The answers to these questions will have implications for real issues in the congregation, like further clarifying the welcome for LGBTQIA+ people, improving the accessibility of the church facilities, and talking about how to combat the challenges of Christian nationalism in our culture.

South Elkhorn's journey is a wonderful testament to the fact that congregations who thrive understand who they are called to be *in this time* and *in this place.* They know that the church they were twenty-five, ten, and even five years ago may not be who they're called to be now. Thriving churches have a seemingly endless desire to align themselves with God's calling. They do this with statements that guide them and shape the types of ministries they offer. But these guiding statements are more than just words on a page or wall; they're tools for discerning how the church will continue to live into their calling.

Values, Mission, Identity: What's the Difference?

Before you can do the work of articulating God's call for your congregation, we think it is helpful to understand the language we use to differentiate between the types of statements. You may be asking, "What's the difference between an identity statement, a mission statement, and a vision statement?" and wondering "Which one should my church use?" Briefly put, the best statement for your congregation is the statement your church needs. Choosing which type of statement is best for you is part of the discernment work of visioning. The terms are different because the statements serve different purposes. So, what do we mean when we refer to a congregation's guiding statements? In our experience, these statements usually exist in one of three forms: *mission statements, identity statements*, and *value statements*.

Mission Statements. These statements illustrate what the congregation seeks to do or be in the larger world. Mission statements can be generic or specific. Some examples are:

- To know God and make God known
- We seek to make Heaven more crowded
- A place to worship God and serve others
- To love God, love the church, love the city, and love the nations

Mission statements are rooted in what the church aspires to do, now and in the future. They are valuable to a congregation because they are short, memorable, and clear. While the statements can provide clarity and theological grounding, they don't always capture the uniqueness of a particular congregation. Some churches call their statement a mission statement, but it is actually an identity statement.

Identity Statements. Identity statements work well for congregations who want to paint a precise picture about who they are, now. They often describe ties to larger denominational organizations or introduce core values, like hospitality or outreach. Identity statements often demonstrate reasons a congregation exists or whom they include.

Some examples are:

> [Our Church] is an open and affirming congregation. We invite all people into community and ministry, regardless of age, race, gender, sexual identity, economic status, faith heritage, or personal ability. We are Disciples of Christ, a movement for wholeness in a fragmented world. You are welcome here!
> [This Church] of Anytown, KY equips every believer through a Christ-centered Gospel to serve as courageous ambassadors in the church, community, and world.

> We are a caring community from various backgrounds, drawn together by the love of God and the transforming message of Jesus. We believe all persons are of sacred worth and dignity without exception—everyone means everyone—regardless of age, race, ethnicity, gender, family structure, marital status, sexual orientation, gender identity, economic background, political affiliation, physical or mental ability, faith history or life experience. We recognize among us differences in theology and biblical interpretation, and we covenant to accept, respect, and love one another on our faith journeys.

Identity statements help the congregation feel that their message is being heard clearly by those who read it or hear it. Unlike mission statements, some identity statements don't roll off the tongue or linger on the ear because of the amount of detail in them. They require more effort on the part of the listener to know what the congregation is about. Some churches will call these vision statements because they are aspirational—who or what the church dreams to be.

Values Statements. Values statements articulate what the congregation values most. Many times, these are quite succinct, sometimes in list form. They serve as a framework around which the congregation can build its programs, outreach, and missional work. In this regard, values statements are somewhere between the role of an identity statement (tell our audience who we are) and a mission statement (declare to the community what we do). Rather, these statements tell the community what matters to us. For example, South

22   THRIVING CHURCH

Elkhorn Christian Church has both a mission statement ("Inspiring Christ's deeper way of love") and a values statement:

OUR VALUES

- Extravagant Welcome
- Real Rest
- Spiritual Resilience
- Courageous Conversation
- Contagious Joy

These statements are broad and strike a balance between vagueness and specificity, leaving room for the congregation to discern how they are best lived out. Words like "extravagant welcome" do not state specifically who is welcomed like an identity statement might, but they make clear to an outsider that the congregation seeks to do more than say hello to a visitor at a Sunday morning worship service. The addition of "extravagant" to the value of welcome tells the hearer to expect more; the value also clearly indicates to the membership of the congregation their responsibility: they are to welcome "extravagantly" those in their midst.

Take Your Time

So, how do you know what kind of statement *your* congregation needs to thrive in living out God's call? We believe your context will help you to answer that question. You may find yourself reflecting on questions like:

- What, if anything, does our surrounding community already know about us?
- Can our membership clearly articulate what it means to be part of this congregation?
- What does this church seek to be and do?
- What is the "personality" of this congregation?

In discerning the type of statement you choose to craft, these and other questions will guide your experience and help you to figure out the most effective process for your congregation. South Elkhorn used the book *Church Unique* by Will Mancini in their process. Other churches in the Thriving Congregations Project used other tools. The important component of building a statement for your congregation is listening well to the congregation.

Listening well requires taking your time. South Elkhorn needed four years to get through their process. Not all congregations need that amount of time, but it is important not to rush the process. Several churches in the Thriving Congregations Project completed their work in six to eight months. Whether your church is able to do the work in a matter of months or a matter of years will depend on your context. Smaller congregations may be able to listen more efficiently; churches in major transition (such as the arrival of a new Senior Minister that South Elkhorn experienced) may need more time to develop relationships and learn from one another. Sometimes the "slow stew" (as Michael called it) is helpful.

Include a Diversity of Voices

Perhaps the most significant driver for understanding a congregation's mission/vision/identity is making sure the right people are in the room to have that conversation. If the pastor is steering the conversation around mission and values, they should be intentional about who is included. Key leaders in the congregation must be a part of this process for the conversation to be considered valuable to the other members. For some congregations, this may be the work of the elders or deacons (or both); for other congregations this may be the board or another governing body. Still others may call together a special team to lead this process. In many congregations, the work team will be a mixture of stakeholders in the congregation, regardless of their title or position. Michael assembled a core team of the board vice moderator, two members at large, and himself as senior minister. He then created a wider network of conversation partners that included the elders, staff members, and other key stakeholders in the congregation.

We suggest the leader ask this question, "If I assemble this group of people, whose voices are missing?" Depending on the congregation,

24   THRIVING CHURCH

it may or may not be prudent to add those additional voices to the conversation, but at minimum it's helpful for the team to be aware of their absence. For example, one congregation we have studied asked their elders to lead the visioning process. At the time, the elder body consisted of a mother/son duo with decades of membership in the congregation, two lifelong members, the pastor's spouse, a newer member from a marginalized community, and a married couple with significant influence in the community. This group largely reflected the diversity of the congregation at the time. However, it was missing anyone younger than forty years old. The congregation did not feel it was necessary to recruit a member to serve who was under forty, but it was important to name that such voices were absent from the initial conversations. In order to compensate for their absence among the elders, two listening sessions targeted those under forty: one for high school and college students, and a second one for parents of young children. It was important to that congregation that they hear the thoughts of these two groups specifically.

Resist the Shelf

One thing that differentiates a thriving church from a congregation struggling to thrive is its ability to live into the things they discern about themselves. Many churches spend months on a discernment process and adopt new statements, only to put everything as it were on a shelf in the pastor's office, never to be touched again. Throughout all of the listening sessions or congregational meetings or other gatherings, the church has heard the members tell them what God is asking of them next. If done correctly, the guiding team has synthesized that information as part of creating a new statement. In so doing, the congregation has learned that God has things in store for them. Whether a hard truth ("we don't need this building anymore to be who God has called us to be") or an exciting new one ("God is calling us to be engaged in feeding our neighbors"), thriving churches invite that calling to permeate their very lives. Rather than give into the fatigue that comes from executing the process, they push through the important step of implementation. They reject the idea that a catchy new slogan means that the work of visioning is already finished. Instead, they pursue the projects the congregation most needs to tackle.

The thriving church begins, even before discernment is finished, thinking about how this will change the way the church operates. For South Elkhorn, the process produced more than a new color and words on a page. Shortly after the congregation voted to adopt the new vision and mission, Michael preached a sermon series on it, painting a picture for how the statements would come to life in the congregation. In addition, Michael notes that as the congregation has prepared to make important decisions, it appeals to some of the values it had articulated earlier as being central to its calling. For example, the value of "courageous conversation" has inspired the congregation not to shy away from the more challenging parts of being a church family together.

Thus, thriving churches *use* what they've learned from their discernment process to create a new way of being church. It may be that the church's governing structure needs to be revisited after a visioning statement; it may be that ministries the church has long held are due for retirement; or it may be that the congregation finds a way to partner with a new organization in town. Whatever the case, we hope your new statements will lead you into an exciting new future.

Write "in Pencil"

Thriving churches seek to understand who they are and who God is calling them to be in this time and this place. Building guiding statements that root the congregation on solid ground provides the congregation with a framework for discovering the next faithful steps in the journey. Congregations like South Elkhorn demonstrate that even churches that are over 250 years old can grow into a new understanding of themselves. After all, we serve a God who is always on the move, always calling us to do new things for the kin-dom. It may seem that you finally reach a clear understanding of your mission and then God calls you to something new. That's OK. Write your statements "in pencil," knowing that God will guide you every step of the way, even through repeated changes. Allow the Holy Spirit to nudge you to change as you continuously discern where God is calling you next.

South Elkhorn is living out its mission and values because its calling is clear to more than just the pastor and staff members; the people in the pews understand who they are and why they exist where they do. They are a church on the move, rooted in their historic location and looking toward their future. South Elkhorn is a congregation using its new tools to guide its ministry and frame its participation in God's world.

The Bible is clear that a vision gives God's people a roadmap for how to be faithful followers seeking to do God's will on earth. Proverbs 29:18 states it plainly, "Where there is no vision, the people perish" (KJV). A call to be God's ambassadors in this world is the overarching narrative for a gathering of believers. Their next step is to figure out what that means for them in their particular time and place, contextualizing the timeless word of God calling them to God's work. But the Proverbs passage is clear: without a clear sense of who they are called to be, God's people will not thrive.

Jesus models this in the fourth chapter of Luke when he cites the prophet Isaiah as his own personal mission statement. These words become the marching orders for Jesus and his followers as they bring the good news to those around them:

"The Spirit of the Lord is on me,
because he has anointed me
to proclaim good news to the poor.
He has sent me to proclaim freedom for the prisoners
and recovery of sight for the blind,
to set the oppressed free,
to proclaim the year of the Lord's favor."

Scriptures to Study

- Proverbs 29:18
- Habakkuk 2:2–3
- Luke 3:1–6

QUESTIONS FOR REFLECTION

1. Jesus is clear about his mission in Luke 4, citing passages from the prophet Isaiah. What scriptures frame the values your congregation holds?

2. What is your church's current mission? When was the last time it was reviewed? Does it still feel relevant? How, or why not?

3. Proverbs says, "Where there is no vision, the people perish." How does your mission help your congregation thrive?

4. What are the next steps your congregation will take to ensure that the work of clarifying its mission continues? How will it "resist the bookshelf"?

Thriving Congregations Understand Community and Rest

The Story of Daytona Beach Drive-In Christian Church, Daytona Beach Shores, Florida

It is not unusual for new church starts to worship in peculiar places: a strip mall store front, an elementary school cafeteria, even the auditorium of a movie theater. At least the last option has built-in seating and a screen for projecting song lyrics. Popcorn for communion, anyone? But there is one type of movie theater experience that would seem to be antithetical to a community-building worship service.

Yes, the name of the church in this chapter's title is correct. And yes, these people do worship in an old drive-in movie theater, a space that has been repurposed from reel-to-reel to real life encounters with God. No, there is no longer a screen. Yes, people worship from their cars (although you can also worship from the chapel, one of the benches placed around the property, or online). Yes, they celebrate communion weekly. And, most importantly, yes, they are thriving.

Daytona Beach Drive-In Christian Church (known locally as "The Drive-In Church") has been around for seventy years, first started in 1953 as a mission opportunity to meet the needs of seasonal residents and vacationers in the highly popular destination of Daytona Beach, Florida. That mission is still a part of The Drive-In Church's soul, which means their congregational demographics do not fit into any conventional church attendance graphs. The worshipping community varies from week to week, but it is typical for 15 percent of attendees to be visitors and vacationers. Demographically, the congregation is diverse and has an average age of around sixty.

30   THRIVING CHURCH

The senior minister, Rev. Bob Kemp Baird, followed a long-tenured pastor when he came to the church in 2012. Bob and his wife, Linda, had worshipped at the church a few years previously at the invitation of the then-senior minister. He says he found the experience to be "unique, a bit quirky," but that he found that "the worship was vibrant, thoughtful, and inspiring, and [that] the people were warm and genuinely welcoming, even asking when we were relocating to Florida."

Whether that question was coincidence or providence, it proved prescient. Bob interviewed for the senior minister position at The Drive-In Church and found a continuation of his first experience. He says, "These traits [that he experienced on his first visit] were a part of the DNA of this congregation, clueing me in on the truth that these people really work at this." The church was poised for new leadership and, under Bob's guidance, worked toward the identified goals of numerical and spiritual growth, updates to the campus, and continued community engagement. A few years later, the church hired an associate minister, Rev. Melissa Frantz, who had the distinction of having grown up at The Drive-In Church. She says, "I have both long-term and short-term relationships with those who worship and participate in the life of the church and have found them willing to try new things [in ways that are] a bit easier than other contexts may experience."

The questions raised about a church existing in a drive-in movie theater setting go far beyond logistics. The sense of community is an integral part of a congregation as people build relationships, share sacred space, work together on ministry teams and committees, and offer compassionate care. On a typical Sunday morning at The Drive-In Church, there's ministry taking place all over its ten-acre property. How do you accomplish this when worshippers are mostly siloed in their own vehicles? How do you encourage informal connections and parking-lot conversations (the healthy kind) when your whole worship space is a parking lot?

One benefit unique to The Drive-In Church is the novelty of the setting. "The fact that we are an outdoor church by the ocean offers a unique opportunity for worship that is a draw for many to give it a try," says church member Rich Lee. But getting them in the door (or, in this case, the driveway) is not enough to convey a sense of the community. A thriving church recognizes its obstacles to building community and has a plan for addressing them.

Bob and Melissa are keenly aware of these challenges each Sunday. Bob says,

> When you are as isolated as worshipers at The Drive-In Church are during the worship time, and there's an opportunity to come and go without having to greet or be greeted by anyone, you have to go out of your way to get to know each other. And you have to go further out of your way to care about each other and show compassion toward one another.

Melissa says that one of the keys for The Drive-In Church leaders is messaging. "In Sunday morning worship we are careful in our announcements, as well as in the liturgical flow of the service, to make sure that people feel included and appreciated." The staff of The Drive-In Church are mindful of the different contexts in which people are experiencing the worship service and make sure that the message is clearly communicated through all the modes of delivery, from an FM radio to a computer screen, to the five hundred to six hundred weekly worshippers (eight hundred to nine hundred during snowbird season).

While some might see the setting of worship as a detriment, there are benefits—on which the church has capitalized. One testimonial from the church's website says, "'Come as you are in your car' leaves you no excuses." Another notes, "We bring our dog, which is always welcomed with open arms and dog treats." And a third calls The Drive-In Church a "feel-good house of worship," which is interesting since this house has no walls, no doors, and no roof.

But as thriving churches know, worship is only one of the ways in which community is built. Churches with multiple worship services can find themselves with sub-congregations within their larger one, depending on which service people attend or whether they worship in-person or online. A thriving church transcends these divisions by providing ample opportunities for people to come together in fellowship, education, and service, strengthening their connections to each other.

Because of the uniqueness of The Drive-In Church's existence, this is an ongoing challenge for Bob and Melissa. "We are experimenting with enhancements to our website as well as the development of an app-based community," says Melissa. "In addition, we are endeavoring to meet the needs of a growing online worshipping community by offering other online opportunities to grow and serve." Many churches face this challenge today, but thriving ones are providing ways for online worshippers to connect, participate, and give.

A quick glance at The Drive-In Church's website paints a vibrant picture of a church that genuinely enjoys being together. In the photo gallery, only a handful of pictures are of the worship service. Instead, most of them are of groups of people learning, laughing, playing, and serving together. For example, the church's small-group ministry provides a variety of ways for people to connect through worship, study, prayer, fellowship, and mission. Under the Connections tab you will find ample opportunities to connect, from regular potluck dinners to quilting circles and from yoga classes to a number of recovery groups.

"Providing opportunities for fellowship and service, as well as opportunities to get out of our cars and gather together becomes vital in order to build community," says Melissa. The congregation's outreach focus includes addressing food insecurity in the Daytona Beach community. The church provides weekly food packages for a nearby elementary school whose students are identified as homeless or near homeless. And a four-night Drive Through Bethlehem experience during the Christmas season not only attracts over two thousand people from the community but engages over fifty congregational volunteers.

This high level of congregational involvement beyond worship points to an important perspective on the part of The Drive-In Church's staff. While congregational leaders like Rich commend Bob and Melissa for their hands-on involvement with the congregation, Bob and Melissa recognize that the responsibility for building community does not fall squarely on their shoulders alone. Although they still greet people as they enter and leave worship, they have recognized that they make a different kind of connection with the congregation on Sunday morning than do churches that have sanctuary doors. Therefore, the staff of The Drive-In Church lean heavily on their lay leaders, who not only reflect the diversity of the congregation, but are also people who are committed to empowering others to participate in the larger church community. Melissa says, "Our pastoral leadership works to identify key leaders with...gifts, talents, and traits that help us to equip one another with opportunities to share those."

"Share" is a keyword in the life of The Drive-In Church and other thriving churches. Pastors of these kinds of congregations recognize that one of their primary pastoral roles is not to do the ministry of the church themselves, but to empower the laity to do it, each person answering their call to serve through the congregation. Even with a congregation as diverse and transient as The Drive-In Church, the shared leadership approach of the staff creates "common unity," as people of different ages, socio-economic statuses, and political parties come together as the body of Christ.

One example of this community building is how the congregation looks out for each other. Recognizing that the ministry to which The Drive-In Church is called extends far beyond the property lines of the church, and that the pastors can only reach so many people each week, the staff started a program called "Care Connect." Melissa says,

> With one pastor-generated email a week, this ministry that began with twelve to fifteen people several years ago has expanded to approximately 100 participants who actively engage in weekly prayer for pastoral needs that we share with them (with permission) and many of them take it a step further to mail cards of care and support.

Church member Sue Jenkins says, "And as someone who had received those cards, that incredible outpouring of love is an amazing experience."

The beauty of this ministry is that it is not simply another program in which people can participate; it's one of the ways in which The Drive-In Church weaves a web of connection among and between its members. Melissa says, "Whether it's for a medical need or to celebrate the birth of a child, this simple ministry has been incredibly powerful in our congregation and is mentioned multiple times a week by people—whether they're offering this prayerful support or are the recipients of it."

It's this kind of ministry that not only builds community, but helps guard against one of the most insidious threats to a church's call to build God's kin-dom. As anyone who has ever thrown themselves into serving God knows, this kind of fervent commitment can come with a dark consequence: burnout. The drive to love God with all our minds, hearts, bodies, and souls can keep us from taking care of ourselves, ignoring the Sabbath commandment in the name of "doing the Lord's work." How do the staff at The Drive-In Church build in time and space to care for themselves?

The answer seems obvious but is often ignored by pastors who feel the pressure to keep their church thriving. "We recognize the importance of preserving our days off, utilizing all the vacation time provided to us, planning for rest and renewal through sabbatical, and engaging in daily spiritual reflection," says Melissa. Too many pastors don't fully use the time allotted to them for rest because there's always one more call to make. To paraphrase Jesus, "The emails will always be with you." If pastors don't take care of themselves, how can they be expected to be effective and engaged in their church's community-building? As leaders of the church, pastors are called to model not only what it means to serve, but also what it means to rest.

Bob admits to feeling the tension between caring for his congregation and for himself. He says, "When I came to the church, I was the only clergy on staff and the only full-time staff person. I also, as head of staff, make sure that everyone is taking their day off and using their vacation time, so I have gotten better at setting an example and taking mine." While keeping a sabbath week-to-week can be tough, Bob honors his vacation time, even if it only means a trip to a state park in his and Linda's camper trailer.

The Drive-In Church has built this into their lay leadership structure, requiring a one-year sabbatical after three years of service. The church encourages lay leaders not to conduct business on Sunday morning so as not to contaminate the time set aside for worshipping God. And the ministers are mindful that their congregational leaders have lives beyond the church. Melissa says, "We recognize that sometimes when people are going through difficult times that perhaps they need to take a step back from their areas of ministry, and we extend that grace to each other to be able to have a break from the rigor and responsibilities of church leadership." A hallmark of a thriving church that values community is stepping up so others can step back, making sure the yoke of the congregation's ministry is shared.

Rich shares a real-life example of this practice of rest. "I have an active role in one of the church's annual events and I met with (Bob and Melissa) to explain that the current process was too much for myself and other volunteers to complete [in the way we have done it in the past]," he says. "We agreed to spread the work over more time, which allows for more physical rest and allows those interested to help who may not have been available under the old process." The staff's recognition of Rich's need for rest kept him engaged when otherwise he may have burned out.

As Bob and Melissa lead The Drive-In Church into the future, the focus on community-building will be a driving force, shaped by the defining symbol of Christian faith. Melissa says, "Something that our pastors keep in the forefront of the congregation is the imagery of the cross, encouraging the congregation...not only [to] look up, but...also [to] look out. We work hard to remind each other that, as people of faith, we are called to serve the needs of others. This is the seed that we believe allows the community to grow."

36   THRIVING CHURCH

Bob echoes this commitment to community. "We continue to be intentional about creating community out of separateness, celebrating unity even when we are distant or remote, and extending grace, compassion, and hospitality as the gifts of God that bind us together even when we are far apart." In a thriving congregation, community transcends socially-built boundaries—even those created by the very cars we drive.

True Community

When you think about community, what comes to mind? For us children of the 1970s and 1980s, it looks a little bit like Mr. Rogers' Neighborhood: A cozy little home on a quiet suburban street where the mailman, trash collector, and other helpers are known by name and by their story. They are friends, not just transactional partners. On Mr. Rogers' TV show, even the puppets aren't afraid to be vulnerable in order to make a connection!

While the congregational community rarely looks anything like Mr. Rogers' Neighborhood, perhaps there are lessons from that fictional world that can help a church thrive.

Community is intentional. Mr. Rogers goes out of his way to ask Mr. McFeeley, the mailman, about his day and then he listens intently. His kind tone and warm demeanor give Mr. McFeeley the opportunity to respond without feeling rushed or dismissed. We're sure Mr. Rogers has plenty of other things he has to get done that day (those cardigans don't wash themselves!), but he takes the time to interact with those around him, showing genuine interest in them.

There are plenty of people all around us every day who are longing to be seen and to share the image of God within them. Like Moses at the burning bush, we have to be intentional about turning aside to acknowledge them.

Community is place-based. Mr. Rogers doesn't go on any flights to other countries. Rather, he befriends the people right in his neighborhood. "They're the people that you meet when you're walking down the street." For a congregation like The Drive-In Church, which literally has members from all fifty states, place-based community looks a little different than it did for Fred Rogers. But, despite both the diversity and transience, The Drive-In Church is very much rooted in its neighborhood. The ministries of this church are focused on meeting the tangible needs of those around them, and relationships between the congregation and the Daytona Beach community have deep roots. When the traveling snowbirds go home for the summer, their offering dollars still do God's work in Volusia County. When people attend board meetings, the topics of discussion involve the church's beachside property and events to be held on site. While some members may be away from Daytona for a while, they call the church their "home church" for a reason—because their community is based here. The COVID-19 pandemic taught us that we can be physically absent from one another and still rooted in a place. Some congregations view digital and distant participants as less significant to the life of the church, but thriving churches know that place-based community does not have to be limited by geography. Some congregations see the digital realm as the enemy of community, causing true relationships to break down. Perhaps, though, the ability to connect even when your body cannot be physically present is the newest way to be in meaningful relationships.

Community is reciprocal. There will always be an inherent disparity of power between employees of a congregation and volunteers. However, thriving churches live out their community in partnership. Lay leaders share not only responsibility but relationships with their staff, and the staff know the work will not be done effectively without the input and energy of the laity. An egalitarian structure creates a healthy dynamic that enables staff and laity to care for one another, as The Drive-In Church does with its Care Connect ministry. No individual part of the body is less or more important than another. Mr. Rogers never tells the garbage collector, "You're just here to take my trash; now be on your way." Mr. Rogers stops to ask him about his family, genuinely interested in how his children are growing up and what his life is like. Mr. Rogers demonstrated to an entire generation that talking about your feelings is an important part of life,

38 THRIVING CHURCH

but listening is an equally important part. In so doing, he modeled reciprocal community. He understands the need for reciprocal relationships with those in his community.

Building Community

The truth of the matter, though, is that none of us, not even our churches, gets to live in Mr. Rogers' Neighborhood. We are busy people interacting with busy people. In our society, the mailman doesn't have time to stop at each house and enjoy a porch conversation about life. Congregations are full of people rushing from one thing to the next, sometimes at the cost of real relationships. How, then, does a congregation successfully build community?

Authenticity. Many denominations encourage pastors to keep a professional distance from their lay leaders. While boundaries are supremely important, hiding your entire personal life from the laity means they will never know the authentic you. While exercising caution when employing church members to do personal work is a prudent endeavor, that doesn't mean you should avoid seeing them outside the church walls. Should you hire a church member to install a floor in your home? Probably not. But should you have lunch out with your family and another family after worship? Probably! Just make sure you divide your time equally among members of the congregation. You don't want to be seen as having "favorites," but you also don't want to seem aloof and uninterested in the members of this body you are called to shepherd. After all, Jesus says, "I know my sheep." and you can get to know them a lot better when the meals you share together extend beyond the communion table and the fellowship hall.

The same is true among the laity. If we spend our time and energy making ourselves look as good as possible to one another, brushing off the dust and polishing our rough edges, we never develop authentic relationships with one another. We only know each other at a superficial level: "That's Lindsey with her two kids and spouse. I think she's a schoolteacher and he's a doctor." How will knowing just those things help us to build relationships with one another that foster community? We have to be authentic, which requires vulnerability, with one another if we want to deepen our relationships. "How are you?" should never be asked in a church unless the asker intends to listen to the answer, and a response of "Fine, how are you?" keeps our relationships superficial. "How are you?" is met with an honest answer in authentic relationships such as, "I've had a busy week at work, and my spouse has had to work overtime; we are all a little out of sorts today." Even this level of vulnerability begins to build a relationship. Over time, these moments of vulnerability pave the way for rich and lasting relationships that support us in the hardest times.

Courage. Vulnerability requires courage. As lay leaders and as clergy, we must act bravely when given the opportunity to share. We find our similarities and our differences when we are vulnerable with one another. If none of us is brave enough to say, "Here's my true story—the unedited version," we will never grow as a community. Members of The Drive-In Church take the step of faith outside their vehicles to eat together, serve together, and spend time together. Not only do they get to know each other at a deeper level, they build shared memories together.

Fun. The congregation that plays together, that laughs together, that enjoys being with one another, will deepen its sense of community. When was the last time your church had a semi-spontaneous fun event? "Anyone who wants to come, we're going to show a movie on the side of the building on Friday. Bring a chair and a snack to share!" Often, congregations run the risk of planning the fun out of an event. We try to make sure the movie has a theme we can discuss, or a mission project attached in partnership with the movie such as, "Donations will be accepted for Habitat for Humanity." While these are necessary and important parts of the life of the church, what if—on occasion—the only purpose was to have some fun together?

Shared Purpose. Community grows when people join together for a common cause. We see this in political rallies, at sporting events, in local service projects and mission trips, in classroom experiences, and so many other places. Where people gather with a singular purpose in mind, community is built.

One congregation learned to share their stories over the course of a church clean-up day. As closets were emptied and shelves sorted, the members, working shoulder to shoulder, began to tell stories about why certain items were in the building. Newer participants in the life of the church were sometimes right next to lifelong members.

"This is a strange sign. Where was this used?"

"Oh! We used to have teams in the local basketball league and these were the banners we made when our team made the playoffs!"

While the signs were no longer needed and could be let go, people shared stories of the life of the church while preparing the building to make new stories and memories.

Rest as a vital part of community

Thriving congregations understand rest as a significant part of building community with one another. They see rest not merely as a break for an individual, but also as a time when new leaders emerge and are encouraged to flourish in roles they may never have explored on their own.

Lay leaders need rest from their work in congregations at least as often as pastors do. Unlike full-time clergy, many lay leaders also manage their own full-time jobs. The work they do for the congregation is time they are happy to donate to the church, but they have to do so around their professional and personal lives. And yet nearly every congregation has lay people who have carried significant leadership roles for decades. How long has your loyal Sunday School teacher been leading that class? How long has the person who makes the coffee been arriving an hour early on Sundays to make sure it's ready? The sabbath mandate was so important it made God's Top Ten list. Who in your church leadership needs to rest?

Erin was recently in a congregation that celebrated a man who had been their Sunday School Coordinator (a volunteer position) for fifty years. This well-meaning congregation rejoiced in the fact that Mr. Jeff had barely missed a Sunday in half a century. As she listened to the love and admiration they had for Mr. Jeff and his selfless service

Thriving Congregations Understand Community and Rest 41

of the congregation, she wondered how different that responsibility might be if Jeff had been encouraged to take a year off every now and then. Would Jeff have discovered a new passion? Would a young adult have taken up the mantle of leadership, only to find her sense of calling in Faith Formation?

While Jeff's gift of his time to the congregation he loves is noteworthy, the congregation did not encourage him to rest from his work as Sunday School Coordinator. Because Jeff continues to serve in this role without time off, the congregation still does not know if Jeff's ministry could be positively impacted by a period of rest. The healthiest of thriving churches might have done this differently.

Elements of rest

Psychologist and author Allaya Cooks-Campbell claims there are seven kinds of rest. The reason we often don't feel rested is because we don't honor all seven types of rest our body needs[1]. Cooks-Campbell cites Dr. Saundra Dalton-Smith[2], who claims we need physical rest (sleeping, sitting still, etc.), creative rest (time to make things), mental rest (disconnection from cognitive demands), social rest (time with relationships that nourish you), emotional rest (setting firm boundaries), sensory rest (turning down sensory inputs like screens, music, lights, and ambient noise), and spiritual rest (time for worship and belonging).

Rest is an essential part of the life of a community. Even God takes time to rest. We are, in fact, *commanded* to rest as God rests. To power through our lives as if we do not need rest is to be disobedient to this command from God. You cannot go through life only inhaling; at some point you have to exhale. Thriving congregations know when to encourage their leaders to stop and take a breath. When pastors and lay leaders do not honor rest, they are setting themselves up for fatigue,

---

[1] For a detailed analysis of this, see her article *Seven Types of Rest (Because You Need More Rest in Your Life)* published on psychcentral.com.

[2] (https://www.ted.com/talks/saundra_dalton_smith_the_real_reason_why_we_are_tired_and_what_to_do_about_it?utm_campaign=tedspread&utm_medium=referral&utm_source=tedcomshare)

42 THRIVING CHURCH

exhaustion, and even burnout. The best way to combat burnout is through regular observance of real rest.

The Drive-In Church has natural rhythms of rest for many of their lay people. Those who spend part of the year in Daytona and part in other places "up north" come and go through the life of the congregation during the year, giving them physical time away from the demands of lay leadership in Daytona Beach. Those who work with children or who teach Sunday School may be away for several months at a time, taking a natural and rhythmic break from their responsibilities. While the congregation is quite intentional about keeping their seasonal members from disconnecting while they are away, the natural rhythm of living hundreds of miles away from the church's campus changes their level of involvement from time to time.

As for the pastoral staff, Melissa is intentional about scheduling her vacation time and her retreat time for the entire calendar year at the beginning of the year. This enables her to plan her times away and protect them. In addition, Melissa always knows how many weeks it will be until her next time of restoration occurs. Finally, by planning her time away a year at a time, Melissa is better able to draw firm boundaries around her protected time of rest. She has the opportunity to tell the congregation "I won't be here on October 10" with a clear boundary that the congregation respects.

Rest as Holy Work

In our productivity-driven world, rest can feel like a waste of time. And yet God calls us to be counter-cultural in the ways we honor the Sabbath and intentionally stop being productive. After all, we are not human doings; we are human beings. At The Drive-In Church, Bob and Melissa do their best to take this seriously, which not only enables them to rest, but also models for the congregation the importance of rest in the rhythm of a life of faith. Melissa says, "Taking time to rest is no longer a luxury for me, but an absolute necessity. [By resting, I] care...for myself, and self-care is critical to the work of long-term ministry." Without rest, The Drive-In Church would be a different congregation. A church with eight hundred people on the roster needs pastors and lay leaders who are well-rested in order to meet needs. Building rest into the culture at The Drive-In Church helps the congregation stay fresh in their work. A thriving church community not only gets a lot done for God's kin-dom but is also comfortable stepping back to do nothing—to the glory of God and of their own souls.

For Study and Discussion

Ever since the observation that it was "not good" that Adam was alone (Gen. 2:18), humanity has been called to be in community with each other. We can do so much more for God when we bring together our gifts to serve each other and the people of God. The early church lived out this understanding, gathering often as the people of God living in community with one another:

All who believed were together and had all things in common; they would sell their possessions and goods and distribute the proceeds to all, as any had need. Day by day, as they spent much time together in the temple, they broke bread at home and ate their food with glad and generous hearts, praising God and having the goodwill of all the people. (Acts 2:44–47)

What started out as a rag-tag group of twelve followers grew into the greatest movement in the world, embodying God's word through relationships and service to God's people.

Scriptures for Study

- Genesis 2:2–3
- Exodus 16:22–30
- Matthew 11:28–30
- Mark 4:35–40
- Acts 2:42–47

QUESTIONS FOR DISCUSSION AND REFLECTION

1. How does your congregation best build community within the church? What can your church do to deepen the relationships between its people?

2. Which lay leaders and/or programs need to rest right now? How can you encourage that in your congregation?

3. Other than pastoral sabbatical, how does your congregation support a healthy work-life balance for your ministerial staff? What can you do to improve those efforts?

4. How can you help your congregation understand the relationship between rest and community? What actionable steps can you take?

Thriving Congregations Reject a Fear Mentality

The Story of Nueva Comunidad Christian Church, Winter Park, Florida

Anyone who's cracked open the Bible or listened to a few Advent sermons knows that the phrase "Do not be afraid" is one of the most prolific in the Bible. Some sources say the phrase appears exactly 365 times—once for each day of the year. Whether or not that is true—and it probably depends on your translation—there's no arguing that the exhortation not to be afraid is one of God's most primary commands.

But, afraid of what? A quick survey shows that when these words are uttered, they usually precede an event which should absolutely strike fear in the hearts of the participants. In the Hebrew scriptures the command, "Do not be afraid" often comes to Israel right before they are about to go into battle or to a prophet preparing to pronounce a word of condemnation on the people. And in the Second Testament, both Mary and Joseph hear the angel say, "Do not be afraid," which is the ancient equivalent of, "Are you sitting down?" For both of them, the news that follows is of a birth that will not only change their lives and the world in which they live, but all of history.

The circumstances in which Rev. Selena Reyes heard "Do not be afraid" may not have been as consequential as Mary and Joseph's, but it was no less life-changing for her. Selena and her family had plenty of reasons to be afraid as she discerned her call to ministry. And yet, her willingness to say, "Here I am, a servant of the Lord" has changed not only her life but the lives of many people in central Florida.

46 THRIVING CHURCH

Selena started Nueva Comunidad Christian Church (Disciples of Christ) in 2017 as a pet project. Selena had pastored before, but when she came to live in Massachusetts, she was divorced and had been out of ministry for a while. When she first arrived, Selena and her daughter Selys looked for a home church but couldn't quite find the right fit. "We kept jumping between an English church and a Spanish church because I could understand the English better, but the songs weren't what we wanted," says Selys. "We never really could find a church that met both of our needs."

Selena echoes the challenge that language provided in finding a church. "(Hispanic churches) try to keep the music closer to our home countries, but as children go to school, they learn English and begin speaking more English," she says. "You're trying to teach the culture to the child, and they become dominant in English and not the previous culture. If you're bilingual, you don't know if you're functioning in English or Spanish. You become diversified in your mind and spirit and everywhere."

While she was investigating what God's next move for her was going to be, Selena moved to Florida with her daughter and second husband. It was there that the Florida regional minister approached her with the idea of starting a new Hispanic church in the area that would have one quality different from any other: this church would be welcoming to the LGBTQIA+ community, a stance not widely accepted in Hispanic churches. The regional leadership in Florida had done some research among Hispanic families to find out what people wanted. Selena said, "What we found was that people wanted a church to be a healing place. Some people wanted to be more welcoming" than was the norm in other Hispanic churches.

This was a burning bush moment for Selena and Selys, who saw the need for such a congregation, but also the challenges that would inevitably come with it. The new church start was fragile and the two didn't want to do anything to disrupt the launch. But the issue took on new significance for Selena and the church when Selys came out as queer. "I was really encouraging my mom, but she was really scared of using me as the church guinea pig," says Selys. "She didn't know how the church was going to react."

After three years, the church was growing and beginning to have conversations about being more openly welcoming—when COVID hit. The church went online and weathered the crisis as best as possible, but Selena was finding that the challenges to the church's identity weren't just pandemic-related. An associate minister who was working with the church was not on board with the idea of the church being welcoming and was starting to oppose Selena's leadership.

Around the time the congregation went back to meeting in person, the established church that was hosting Nueva Comunidad had a memorial on the anniversary of the Pulse nightclub tragedy, where a gunman ended the lives of 49 people in a popular gay nightclub in Orlando in 2016. "The English church had this black tablecloth put over the altar with jars that had floating candles in rainbow-colored waters," says Selys. "My mom mentioned (Pulse) among other tragedies and the associate minister got very upset about the table decoration. That's [when] we started realizing that maybe everyone wasn't on the same page."

And yet, the church was still reaching people. Selena was working with people within the congregation who were welcoming, and the conversations about inclusiveness continued despite the internal strife. And then Selys came out more widely on Facebook which made church members aware. "I remember wondering if people would really love me," Selys says. "What if they love me so much, they can look past it if they are against it? Maybe I can be an instrument of God who helps these people be more welcoming." Selys' coming out had both intended and unintended consequences for Nueva Comunidad. But this moment was a refining fire, helping the congregation to clarify who God was calling them to be. "The worship leader told me, 'Pastor, we're here. I'm supportive of this ministry and I'm welcoming,'" says Selena.

Recognizing the pivotal nature of this moment in the life of the fledging congregation, Selena called a meeting of those still a part of the church to talk about the future. "We came to the meeting and expressed everything and said we needed to have a vote on whether or not we were going to be welcoming," says Selena. Most of their opinions were that the church needed to be welcoming, but there were detractors. Then Selys spoke:

> In a mix of Spanish and English, I was like, "I want to remind you all that I'm bisexual, so we already have a person who is LGBTQIA+ in the community. However you vote affects me directly. If you vote that we can't lead worship or be on the board or whatever, then I can't do those things anymore. I want you to keep that in mind when you vote."

Ultimately, everyone voted "yes" to being a welcoming congregation, with one abstention. "I like to think I moved the dial a little bit," says Selys.

The vote was only the beginning of the conversation. It's one thing to say you'll be welcoming, but how far will you go to live that out? What fears might keep you from fully living into that identity? For Nueva Comunidad, there were no limits. "Would we marry a couple?" Selena asked of the group. "One of the members said, 'Of course we're going to marry them!' It wasn't a discussion at all. That really touched me because they were not only supporting my daughter; they wanted to create a ministry that would touch a lot of people."

The seeds planted that day are producing a harvest as Nueva Comunidad continues on its journey. The church moved to its current location of Winter Park in 2022, nesting in an older, white, exclusively English-speaking congregation. "We do joint services with Winter Park," says Selena. "They have twenty to twenty-five people and are in our bilingual services. They have joined in the bilingual concept and slowly the congregation is growing."

Rey Acevedo is one of those new members. Rey and his family live in Tampa, a two-hour drive from Winter Park. He was looking for a pastor to perform his wedding and happened upon Selena. "I wasn't expecting when I called her that there would be a place for me," says Rey. Rey was a part of a church in Tampa, but because of his job as a hospital chaplain, his attendance was sporadic. "Even when I was in a church, I still didn't feel that connection of welcome." Now, Rey joins Nueva Comunidad's online gathering every Thursday and travels several hours to Winter Park every four to six weeks to be part of the in-person bilingual services.

Reaching new people has been a blessed consequence of Nueva Comunidad's refusal to let fear dictate their path. "We are one of only two Hispanic churches in the denomination that is welcoming," says Selena. While the region has been supportive, Selena still wonders if the more conservative Hispanic pastors in the denomination will accept her and her ministry because she is so strongly committed to it. At a recent national gathering, another pastor brought an openly gay man to a gathering of Hispanic pastors. Selena recalls, "I felt so much that God was talking to my heart and saying, 'I love them, too.' I felt that so strongly!"

That depth of her conviction has led Selena into the realm of advocacy, including creating a support group for people who have been wounded by the "clobber texts"— the passages of scripture some people use to condemn homosexuality. Selys has also created a Facebook group for people who are queer, and the church has scholarship funds available for queer people who are seeking therapy. "And we went to Pride (festival) this year! That was one of my dreams!" says Selys.

Nueva Comunidad is now seeing their willingness to reject fear ripple into the community, far beyond the places they originally intended. A few months ago, Selena changed jobs and began serving a primarily Hispanic population. "I'm seeing LGBTQ+ patients all the time. God is opening doors there. My manager told me we were the only church like this, so it's OK to invite them."

Rey and other congregation members feel God's Spirit moving through Nueva Comunidad. "Pieces are being put together where you don't see it at first. I was just looking to be welcomed. Now here I am!" Rey wasn't aware of the church's open stance when he first joined, but it resonated with his own life. "I have a stepdaughter who recently came out of the closet. Plus, it's my own theology." And even initial detractors are acknowledging the importance of Nueva Comunidad's ministry. The associate minister who left? She now recognizes the need for this ministry and is supportive of the church's work.

As the church moves forward, it will continue to face situations in which it will have to choose faith over fear. Nueva Comunidad is currently in talks with the Winter Park congregation for a potential merger with Selena as the pastor, but that won't come without costs. "I know I'm probably the most hesitant of anyone in our congregation to merge because I'm scared of losing our history," said Selys. "I'm trying to see if there are ways we can honor both of our histories." Selys holds onto a healthy skepticism about the merger, while naming God's role in the process. "I'm trying to be brave and trust that God is creating with us and isn't going to leave us. I don't really believe everything happens for a reason; I just believe everything happens and God helps us make meaning out of the changes."

Selena admitted that not everyone in the Winter Park congregation is on board with the identity of Nueva Comunidad, but that's not deterring her from pursuing this new avenue. "I don't feel fear because I'm here to serve them." She echoes her daughter Selys' trust in God in the midst of the challenges. A denominational leader told her that some churches would reject her for taking this stance. Selena recalls telling her, "I'm Latina and that isn't going to change. They can reject me, but I'm a Disciple, too." Selys adds, "I'm a voice that isn't going to be quiet." "I remember too that Jesus was scared when he knew he was going to be sacrificed. What would Jesus do? He kept going even when he was scared."

Ultimately, Selena, Selys, and the Nueva Comunidad congregation choose to see how God can use them in spite of the reasons they have to be afraid. "We're expectantly waiting to see what God is doing," says Selena. Those words evoke the image of a young girl visited by an angel who told her some amazingly good news about an upcoming birth. For Mary, for Selena, for Selys, for anyone hesitant to follow God's call into the unknown, the message is simple: "Do not be afraid."

Dream with God

What would you do if you were unafraid? The question permeates therapy offices across the United States. Given the opportunity to answer the question in a confidential and safe space, counselors and therapists hear profound answers—answers of longing, answers of dreams fulfilled, answers of hope. The church is made up of pastors, leaders, and laity who live in a culture dripping with fear. In nearly every context, someone is telling us to be afraid—to be afraid of people who do not look like you; to be afraid of the government; to be afraid of what your children might learn; to be afraid of impending disaster; to be afraid of violence. Everywhere we turn, something or someone is keeping us afraid. The church is no different.

What or whom does your church fear? Being ostracized? Being publicly criticized for your beliefs? Losing members? Not having enough money? Change? If it is allowed to do so, slowly and over time, fear can become the dominant emotion inside the walls of a church. It almost seems to be the natural order of a congregation's life—to return to fear when choices arise.

This does not have to be the case. Congregations can build up their resistance to fear as the default emotion. You may be saying, "Well, sure! If all you have to do is start a new congregation, then you don't have to deal with fear." But historic, middle-aged, and new churches all have to walk the same journey with fear. Nueva Comunidad's newness is not what enables them to reject a mentality of fear.

Perhaps the question from the therapists' office needs to be changed just a little bit for churches. Maybe instead of asking "What would you do if you were unafraid?" the question needs to be "What is God's dream for us that feels scary?"

Congregations who dream with God are taking the first step toward rejecting fear. Dreaming together allows churches the opportunity to imagine what God could do. What does it look like to dream together where you are? Depending on your congregational size, maybe it includes a gathering where people are free to express

52   THRIVING CHURCH

their answers without judgment or commentary. Maybe it is a bulletin board where folks can anonymously post their own dreams for the church. Maybe it is a conversation that begins with the Board or the Elders. In whatever way you discern is best for your church, rejecting fear begins with a dream.

For Nueva Comunidad, that dream was to create a safe space for Hispanic people who were LGBTQIA+ or who had family members who were LGBTQIA+. For your church it may be a dream to relocate or to create a ministry that is missing in your community. When God says to your church, "Do not be afraid," what is the statement that follows?

As we mentioned above, God's command not to be afraid often comes right before something that should, in fact, cause us to fear. It's as if God is saying, "Hey, don't be afraid, but I'm calling you to do this scary thing." Churches who are trying to live into rejecting fear answer like Samuel, "Speak, for your servant is listening" (I Samuel 3:10). Samuel hears the words of condemnation on Eli's house. But then Samuel does something unexpected: he lies in his bed, afraid to tell Eli what God has said (3:15). It is not until Eli, Samuel's mentor and friend, encourages him to speak the truth that Samuel gains the courage to do what God has asked of him.

Find Support

Like Samuel, all of us need trusted colleagues who will help us navigate when God calls. Three times God tries to get Samuel's attention; it is Eli who recognizes that God is speaking to Samuel and tells him how to respond. Who in your congregation do you trust with your future? Who do you go to when God calls you somewhere scary?

Part of rejecting fear is having people around you who can encourage you on the journey of faithful progress. Selys needed to tell Selena how Selys' own journey was aligning with Selena's calling to pastor a church for openly queer people. Selys needed the support, but Selys also needed Selena to know Selys had a deeper reason to keep moving forward with the dream—in short, that Selys' theology was also personal. Congregational leaders, whether pastors or laity, need to have trusted people who can help them discern what God may be saying. When God calls, it is important to be able to share God's words with someone who will pray with you, hope for you, and encourage you.

Practice Mindfulness

Mindfulness is the basic ability to be present with our own thoughts. It manifests in many ways—in noticing our breathing, in intentionality around what we eat, in the ways we speak to others. In the case of the church, mindfulness can be a tool to help congregations discern where God is calling them. Nueva Comunidad is a community of faithful participants who talk with one another on a regular basis. The congregation has meetings to talk about their next steps. They work collaboratively with one another to see where God is leading next. They dream together. They work together as they navigate trying times.

Practicing mindfulness in your congregation might look like it does for Nueva Comunidad, or it may look different. Perhaps in your congregation mindfulness looks like a weekly time of prayer over the church's values. Perhaps it looks like a year-long study of scriptures that include the command, "Do not be afraid." It might be a leadership retreat weekend of prayer and fasting. Mindfulness is so highly contextual that it requires leaders to determine what is best for your local church. Whatever it is that you do, the key to mindfulness is to be present with the thoughts of the congregation.

Move with Purpose

As Nueva Comunidad considers a merger with the congregation in Winter Park, the church is navigating those conversations with intentionality. Neither congregation wants to lose their particular and individual history and identity if they should choose to meld into a single congregation. For them, navigating the process has been an exercise in purpose. They are waiting expectantly to see what God will do with both churches as their conversations unfold.

Moving with purpose means the congregation takes intentional steps toward who God is calling them to be. Nueva Comunidad is leaning into its mission to be a welcoming congregation to those often shunned by the Latin church. This church is continuing to work within that calling, even as it also explores where God may be calling it next. Some congregations can lose their sense of purpose while they work on a monumental task, such as a restructure or a merger. Nueva Comunidad is resisting the temptation to ease into complacency while it explores its partnership with Winter Park.

At the heart of its work is Nueva Comunidad's commitment to its mission. The congregation strives to be a community of welcome, and at present that work looks like welcoming a relationship with a congregation vastly different from their own. As the churches lean into their partnership, the leaders of Nueva Comunidad are deliberately trying to honor the heritage of both congregations, to become an even more significant place of welcome.

In your context this may not look like a church merger, but in any scenario it is important to keep the mission at the forefront of your work. Rejecting a fear mentality means moving with purpose to wherever God continues to call you—to the mission and values your church holds dear.

No One is Without Fear

Rejecting a fear mentality does not mean a congregation is fearless. In Nueva Comunidad's story, Selys says, "I know I'm probably the most hesitant of anyone in our congregation to merge because I'm scared of losing our history." Sometimes rejecting fear includes loss…that is the loss of the congregation's previous story, loss of a staff position, loss of a street address, or loss of a once-beloved ministry. To live without a mentality of fear is not to diminish our feelings of fear; rather, it is to live in a way that names the fear and refuses to let it control the actions of the church.

"I'm trying to be brave and trust that God is creating with us and isn't going to leave us," says Selys. Perhaps that is the boldest thing any church can say.

> *The command "Do not be afraid" pervades scripture. Pick just about any story where God is extending a call, and these words are most likely part of it. Sometimes this fear is well-founded (as when a guilt-ridden Adam hides from God in the Garden of Eden), but in most cases God is "en-couraging" (giving courage to) God's fearful people. Abraham, Isaac, Jacob, and Moses all hear these words, but so does the Egyptian servant Hagar, proving that God's comfort knows no boundaries. And Paul summarizes a faithful response to any fearful circumstances when he writes to Timothy, "For God has not given us a spirit of fear, but of power and of love and of a sound mind" (NKJV).*

Texts for Study

- Genesis 15
- I Samuel 3:1–20
- I Chronicles 28:20
- Daniel 3
- Matthew 14:22–32
- Luke 1:26–38

QUESTIONS FOR DISCUSSION AND REFLECTION

1. The Bible has many stories of people whom God encouraged not to be afraid. Which passage (perhaps among those listed above) means the most to you when you are afraid?

2. What would your church do if it were unafraid? What is God's dream for you as a church that feels scary right now?

3. How will you listen for God's calling? What specific plans do you need to put in place?

4. Name a time in your congregation's history when you rejected fear. What was significant about that experience for your church?

5. How can you learn from your church's history to move forward in faith now?

Thriving Congregations
Are Collaborative

The Story of Foothills Christian Church, Phoenix, Arizona

It's a story that church executives know all too well. A downtown church makes the difficult decision to relocate to the suburbs, hoping to find new life on the growing edges of a city. Not everyone goes, and the new church struggles to gain a foothold. The pastor who led the move leaves, and the church muddles through a few interims and ill-fitting pastors as attendance and participation continue to dwindle. Finally, after years of trying to make it work, the church makes another difficult decision, this time to close its doors.

That was almost the story of Foothills Christian Church. The church moved from downtown Phoenix to near Glendale, on the outskirts of Phoenix proper. When it did, it rechristened itself Foothills, as the name Phoenix Central Christian Church no longer fit. Despite the rough start, an enthusiastic pastor and a renewed sense of energy brought Foothills to life, a phoenix rising from the sands of the Arizona desert. Still today, members who were part of the move drive a great distance to be part of the church community.

Foothills is a bit of an anomaly for the area in which it is located. The original plan was for the church to serve the immediate neighborhood that grew up around it, but it has become a destination church, drawing members from across Maricopa County, one of the largest counties in the United States, and from several neighboring towns. Foothills draws membership from all directions, from the South (where Phoenix Central was originally located), and from the West, North, and East. It's just down the road from Christ's Church of the

58   THRIVING CHURCH

Valley, the largest church in Arizona, which has over twenty thousand worshippers monthly across seven campuses. And yet, Foothills is thriving, largely due to a distinct identity in the northern part of the Phoenix valley that sets it apart.

Church member Linda Immel says, "A friend of mine was talking to a friend and told her we were there (Foothills), and she said, 'Oh, the gay church!' So, I guess we're known that way." Indeed, Foothills' decision in 2011 to become open and affirming clarified a core value and solidified its identity, one that it wears with pride and proclaims with courage. For example, when you drive by Foothills on Happy Valley Road, you'll see a prominent set of doors, painted in the colors of the rainbow, which proclaim, "God's doors are open to all."

Foothills' clarity about who it is and whom it serves has been a catalyst for the church's growth. "I think it brings in a lot of people who want to be in an open community," says church member Don Bryant. "One of the things people say is, 'We came here because we wanted a church [that] would show a sense of openness and love for our kids.'" When Linda and her husband, Terry, were looking for a church after relocating from Chicago, they wanted a congregation committed to welcoming all. When they learned that Foothills was going through the open and affirming process, they knew they had found a home. "We joined the first Sunday we attended," says Terry Immel. Pastor Bekah Krevens estimates that at least 30 percent of the congregation are members of the LGBTQIA+ community.

Foothills' open and affirming stance not only sends a message about who is welcome, it also provides a way for them to connect with organizations that share similar values, which was crucial to Foothills' survival. "We are in a mainline Protestant desert," says Bekah. Without similarly minded churches around them with whom to work, Bekah and the Foothills congregation have had to seek out other organizations as ministry partners.

That spirit of collaboration is a hallmark of thriving congregations. Rather than only turning inward for both ideas and volunteers (a practice which can easily burn out an engaged laity), Foothills is constantly seeking ways to put their resources to use to serve the surrounding area. "We are in an affluent suburb," says Bekah, "so we look to support other ministries," rather than Foothills expending energy to start something new.

The breadth of Foothills' collaboration with other organizations and ministries is impressive. They do the typical things of a thriving church, like opening up their building to outside groups on a regular basis. "If you drive by the church any day of the week, you'll see a lot of cars in the parking lot," says church member Linda Siegwald. "We look like the busiest church on the planet!" But the ways in which the church building is used go beyond your typical Boy Scouts and Alcoholic Anonymous meetings.

Siegwald says, "We have times where our Muslim neighbors use our space for Ramadan. We had a Korean church that met in our sanctuary for several years." Bekah adds, "A Hindu community meets now in our fellowship hall on Saturdays. We've become a popular location for Hindu one-year-old birthday parties." Foothills' open and hospitable spirit to a wide range of groups, organizations, and faiths is indicative of its willingness to be a good neighbor, whether that neighbor worships the same god or not.

That desire to collaborate is the lens through which Foothills views all its ministries. "We needed to connect with our neighborhood, so we considered a traditional block party, but we quickly realized it wouldn't work," says Bekah. "We took inventory of who we had relationships with. So, instead we had a multicultural festival focused on a shared value we had with other groups. As it grew over a few years, we refined the focus even further and created a 'connection to nature' event because it was a shared value among all of the groups involved." The neighborhood festival has turned into an annual event and has increased Foothills' ties to the surrounding area.

Foothills' willingness to collaborate with other organizations springs from of the tone Bekah and the other ministerial staff set. Instead of hoarding resources and gate-keeping ideas, the leaders at Foothills encourage members of the congregation to pursue their

60   THRIVING CHURCH

passions in ways that align with the church's mission, as stated on their website, to "love God, serve others, and welcome everybody."

"Foothills is a very permission-giving church," member Linda Sexton says. "If you have an idea, make it happen! Doesn't matter who you are in the church, if it's something that will interest more than just you, put it out there and see if there's interest, and then go with it." Terry adds, "I think there's also a permission to let go. [Just because] we've been doing this for so long doesn't mean we can't let it die."

This willingness to open-source service ideas has led Foothills in a number of exciting and meaningful directions. When asked how the church collaborates, the answers from the laypeople shot up like popcorn. Working with Lutheran Social Services of the Southwest on refugee resettlement, partnering with another local church to provide a cooling center during the sweltering Arizona summer, providing backpacks for children from the Navajo nation, working with the Arizona Faith Network and Arizona Interfaith Power and Light: this is just a sample from the buffet of ways Foothills partners with other agencies to serve.

Part of what makes their collaborations so successful, says Bekah, is that Foothills doesn't collaborate in order to make a name for itself. "We don't care about taking credit when we collaborate with other groups," she says. For instance, the church had planned to have a booth at the Phoenix Pride Festival, but the festival had become so popular and booths so hard to come by that they weren't able to get one. "So, instead we partnered with an organization that serves LGBTQIA+ youth and we put our money into their effort," says Bekah. "We didn't need it to be Foothills' name, we just wanted to be supportive of their work."

A thriving church doesn't have to call attention to itself. Rather, it uses its resources to point to the work of the living Christ in its midst. Another example of Foothills' humility in its approach to collaboration is its work with CASA builders, a denominational effort to build a church and houses in Nogales, Mexico, just across the Arizona border. Over its decades-long involvement in this effort, Foothills has invested thousands of dollars and members have made dozens of trips to Nogales, but not once has it asked for its name to be lifted up. "We don't do that, we don't care if that happens," says Bekah.

And yet, people take notice. Thriving congregations that seek collaboration can't help but be attractive to people who are looking to build difference-making relationships. While the goal of collaboration is not evangelism, it can bring in people who might not otherwise step inside the sanctuary for worship. "Our outreach efforts are open to people who may not be looking for a church home, but they want to be part of what we're doing," says Bekah. She talked about an after-worship sandwich-making service project that was planned and publicized on the church's Facebook page, Nextdoor, and Eventbrite. When worship ended, there were several neighborhood members who had shown up to help.

That's not unusual for a church like Foothills, a progressive point of light in a staunchly conservative community. As people become disenchanted with the theology and values of the evangelical churches in the area, Foothills becomes a natural and welcoming place for them to start or continue their faith deconstruction. The folks at Foothills are trying to reclaim the word "evangelism" with their steady witness, their faithful presence, and their unswerving commitment to let their core values shine acts as a beacon to those in the community looking for a place of acceptance and belonging.

Foothills' clarity about its identity not only encourages ongoing collaboration, but it also helps the church be nimble enough to respond to time-sensitive requests. When the movie "1946: The Translation that Shifted Culture" was on tour, Bekah wanted Foothills to be supportive. The movie focuses on the addition of the word "homosexual" to the 1946 Revised Standard Version of the Bible, which was one of the foundations of the anti-gay movement in America. "I emailed them to find out how we could help," Bekah reports, "and they said, 'Can you host it?'"

With only a few weeks to get ready, the congregation sprang into action, lining up housing for crew members, providing food and hospitality, and opening the doors to those who came to watch the film. "Some of our newest members have come because they first came to that," says Bekah. "Because we knew our values, I didn't have to go to the board for permission."

That clarity of values and mission enables Foothills to enter collaborations boldly, trusting that, no matter who they are working alongside, God is present in the partnership. Rather than seeing people of other faiths or of no faith as a threat, Bekah sees them as opportunities to bond over shared values. "This is a church [that] celebrates who they are," she says. "Before I came, the church had gone through a story of resurrection. Now, this church is a place that is celebrating where they are right now. It's an exciting place to be."

The thriving church is a place that understands the value of collaboration. Foothills Christian Church demonstrates that calling both internally and externally. Their spirit of working together happens inside the building and outside the building, creating partnerships between their members and community organizations around them.

Internal Collaboration

Throughout the Pauline letters, the author uses the body as a metaphor for the church. He uses it to explain the work of the church. In the letter to the Colossians, our internal collaboration (sharing, living in harmony, being grateful) is the key element that holds the church together. It is a challenge for many (actually probably *all*) congregations to live together in unity, and yet the New Testament repeatedly calls us to such behavior.

We believe that this mentality of living together in harmony is the key to internal collaboration. As we will see with external collaboration, internal collaboration requires setting aside our pride to pursue the purposes to which God has called us. Leaders of ministries, teams, committees, and other organizations within the life of the church have to be ready to set aside traditions and name recognition to promote the greatest good.

Asking Good Questions

Like living out the traits lifted up in this book, the work of the collaborative church requires us to ask good questions. The church that wants to work collaboratively inside the walls of the building explores what the congregation most needs at the time. This might mean that the choir needs to take a break from singing so that instrumentalists have an opportunity to lead in worship. It might mean that the board has to relinquish some of its power over the work of committees. It might mean that the fellowship committee and the education committee need to work together to create an experience for the congregation that is fresh and different. The church will never know what the need of the church is if it does not ask good questions.

Good questions are open-ended. They call those who are reflecting to think more expansively than they normally do. Questions might include things like:

- What ministry feels as if it is flat right now? What might be causing that flatness?
- What do we feel God is calling us to do in this season?
- What gifts do some of our folks have that we are not using?
- Who feels left out of leadership right now?

The questions your church is asking are the most important piece of being a collaborative congregation. Without good questions, the church cannot find new answers.

Imagine what might happen in your church if you spent only half of one board meeting exploring the question, "What is God calling us to do in this season?" You might discover together that several members of the board have been feeling a tug to minister to the college students in town. Or you might find that God has been leading your members to be a more deeply praying church, praying each week specifically for members of the congregation. God might reveal any number of things to you in this session!

But if all you do is imagine it, then collaboration is still not happening. Collaboration happens when we move beyond our imagination into the *doing* of the work. So perhaps your board recognizes that your church members need deep, intentional prayer right now. If the board just says, "Make sure you pray for Pam," there's no collaboration happening. Instead, perhaps the board says, "Let's get together some people who like to pray, and some people who like to write cards, and some people who enjoy making phone calls to discover how they might meet this need in our congregation." Collaboration is born in the moment the board *does* something about the need it perceives.

External Collaboration

In many congregations, internal collaboration is easier when it comes to setting aside our pride. It matters less who came up with the idea for the praying ministry; it matters more that people feel supported and prayed for. But when it comes to partnering with external groups, suddenly most churches want their name publicly attached to the work.

We are not opposed to churches getting credit for the work they do. In a culture that is more and more secularized, churches need to make sure that the public knows they exist and what they support. The difference is that the thriving collaborative church does not go into that work *for the purpose of* the publicity. They go into the work because they know that God is moving there, and they want to participate in God's mission for the world.

Foothills decided that a neighborhood block party was not the way to get people onto their campus in hopes of attracting visitors to worship. The goal was for individual people to meet their neighbors. Now members of the church (who may or may not be geographical neighbors with the folks who live near the church) go out of their way to introduce themselves to other people for the purpose of getting to know them. The church members are seeking to find out the priorities of people who live in the neighborhood. Foothills members wanted to know who lives near them, what they celebrate, how they worship (if they do), and what their struggles are. In knowing their neighbors, they were better able to know where they need to partner.

All of Phoenix is dangerously hot in the summer, including the area in northern Phoenix metro. Foothills lacks the physical space required to house a cooling center in their neighborhood. Larkspur Christian Church, however, has the space to host the center. Foothills supports the ministry of Larkspur by preparing sandwiches for the guests who come in to get out of the heat. More than likely, the six thousand people who pass through Larkspur's doors over the course of a summer to stay cool and enjoy a sandwich have no idea that a different church is providing the food. Foothills is fine with that. Jesus never tells us to feed people because we want them to come to our church on Sunday morning. He just tells us to feed them. The people of Foothills are leaning into their partnerships in a way that strengthens their bonds with the people of Larkspur and of the broader neighborhood.

Permission Giving

The most powerful thing a church can do to encourage collaboration is to build an internal network that creates a permission-giving atmosphere. When ministries or committees or small groups of individuals feel empowered to try something without having to get permission from the pastor, the Board, or the congregation, energy is generated. Many collaborative churches also need to be nimble; needs arise quickly that need attention. If members have to go through a long process before the work can begin, sometimes the need has passed by the time the church is ready to consider it. Bekah mentioned that she did not need to seek the Board's permission to volunteer the church as a viewing location for *1946*, because she knew the organization bringing the film and the film itself were in line with the congregation's values.

If your church has strict policies around how actions can take place—particularly urgent ministries—it may be time for your congregation to explore those polices more intentionally. Why were these policies put in place? What happened to create such strict regulations? Do these regulations still need to be in place? If so, why? It may be the case that your policies can be revisited to allow for

66 THRIVING CHURCH

permission with parameters. Perhaps your congregation needs to say, "Anything that costs the church less than $500 can proceed without board approval." Or maybe your policy can say, "If at least five people want the ministry to happen and it aligns with the church's values, the board does not have to approve the decision." The options are endless and contextually specific! It may be that these policies were put in place because the congregation has a history of policy abuse, and that threat remains. If so, this may not be the right time to relax your policies. However, more often than not the risk is lower than the congregation fears.

Wherever the Work is Happening

Thriving congregations know that the work of God is done by people all over the world, whether they know they are doing God's good work or not. They know that the most important thing is not who gets the credit, but that people experience God at work. When these churches invest their time, energy, and resources in true collaboration, they may sometimes be recognized for that work (like Foothills was when they hosted the movie), but at other times they may not be (like when it built homes in Nogales). Regardless, people who otherwise may not have benefited from the ministry that Foothills is uniquely gifted to do were able to reap the blessings of God's goodness lived out. Thriving churches actively look for God at work and seek to join in—wherever the work is happening.

> *"Two are better than one, because they have a good return for their labor," says the writer of the book of Ecclesiastes. Just we are called to be in community, we are called to use that community setting to combine our varied gifts and talents to do God's work. Through the grace of Christ, we are more than the sum of our parts. When we work together—within and beyond the walls of the church—we give the Spirit more room to work.*

Scriptures to Study

- Ecclesiastes 4:9–12
- Romans 12:4–5
- Colossians 3:12–17
- I Peter 4:10

QUESTIONS FOR DISCUSSION

1. Where in your community do you see God at work? What agencies, congregations, religious groups, or social services are doing work that aligns with your church's mission and values?

2. How might your congregation partner with those agencies?

3. What is your congregation currently doing to foster collaboration within your church? How can you be a leader in making that happen more frequently?

4. What scriptural language might your congregation incorporate to foster deeper connections with community partners?

5. "If the work of God is happening, thriving churches want to be part of that work." Is this true for your congregation right now? If not, what is holding you back?

Thriving Congregations Are Generous

The Story of Co-Heirs with Christ Missions, Lexington, Kentucky, and The Story of Second Christian Church, Mayfield, Kentucky

What images come to mind when you think of a generous church? We're guessing that you imagine a congregation that reflects the consumerist culture in which it is embedded. We often equate "generous" with "wealthy," and so we imagine a generous church as one that has vast resources, a sprawling church campus, and a congregation with deep pockets. A generous church probably has a visible steeple that beckons people to it, a freshly paved parking lot for all the members and guests, and a stain-free sanctuary carpet (despite the coffee shop in the church lobby).

Here's what you probably didn't envision: a church started about ten years ago that operates out of a storefront in Lexington, Kentucky, and is bordered by a tobacco shop, a mattress store, and Austin City Saloon. You probably also didn't imagine a generous church as being one that claims about sixty members with around thirty-five in worship each Sunday. And we'll just about guarantee that the generous church you imagined wasn't made up of predominantly African immigrants. When we blow up our expectations of what a thriving congregation *should* look like, we open ourselves to the possibility of seeing thriving churches in the most unlikely of circumstances.

Co-Heirs with Christ Missions (Disciples of Christ) doesn't check any of the traditional "thriving church" boxes, and yet its generosity is exemplary. Started in 2013 by founding pastor Foster Frimpong,

70   THRIVING CHURCH

Co-Heirs claims members who hail from Ghana, Nigeria, Liberia, and Sierra Leone. Worship services are conducted in English with a French interpreter, and often feature lots of singing and dancing, as worshippers embody their unfettered praise of God.

Emelia Agyemang's journey is representative of Co-Heirs members. "I have been a Christian for more than ten years," she says. "I was with the Assembly of God church when I first came to America." After spending time in West Virginia, Emelia and her husband returned to Lexington and joined Co-Heirs because a friend invited her family to church.

Co-Heirs has bucked the trend of new church starts, which rarely make it past the five-year point. In August 2024, Co-Heirs was officially chartered as an established congregation by the Kentucky region of the Christian Church (Disciples of Christ). This means that, after a decade of growing the congregation with the support of the denomination, Co-Heirs is officially on their own, living out their call to serve God in their community.

That call has been instrumental in Co-Heirs' formation. "We believe we're the vessel and the image of God's goodness on earth, bringing goodness in the world. As we believe, we become the hands and feet of Christ in our community," says Foster. In fact, the name of the church comes from the declaration in Romans 8 that, "if we are children, then we are heirs—heirs of God and co-heirs with Christ." The congregation operates with four main "Kin-dom cultures" that it nurtures in its members: reconciliation, care, discipleship, and generosity.

It is this last trait of generosity that has defined Co-Heirs since its beginning and has helped it to buck most new church trends. Foster, himself an immigrant from Ghana, came to America for the specific purpose of going into ministry. His original church start in 2013 split over a number of theological issues, including the role of money in the church. While Foster understood the offering collected was to be used to care for others— "God gives us responsibility with the blessings he gives us"—some in his fledgling congregation were seduced by a prosperity gospel narrative and believed giving to God was a pathway to making themselves wealthy.

Thriving Congregations Are Generous 71

The split happened in 2014, and Foster started Co-Heirs, along with about ten people. But the new church was already beginning with a deficit of $28,000. While many church starts in this kind of crisis turn their resources inward to ensure survival, Foster encouraged his congregation to be a light to the community, especially those new to the country. "Co-Heirs invests in community projects, impacting the lives of the youths and children and also, providing support for struggling families," he says.

For more traditional churches, that might mean writing a check to a local food bank or collecting kitchen cleaning supplies, both of which can be done within the comfort of their church building. But Foster and Co-Heirs is committed to be present in the community in tangible, helpful ways. One powerful example is that the congregation has a transportation fund that supports new refugees and immigrants with hospital appointments and employment for two months to help them get their start-up car. Because they are intimately familiar with the needs of people who are new to their community, they can tailor their generosity to ensure it makes the biggest difference in the lives of those on the receiving end. Emelia says, "I see Co-Heirs as a very generous church. We go beyond our members to the community." Foster echoes this focus beyond the walls of the church when he says, "We believe that our giving will support the impact we will make in the community."

Co-Heirs is able to live out their culture of generosity despite not having the resources of a more established church. Apart from two fundraising efforts to support local families, the church has never conducted a capital campaign. On Sunday morning, church members hear stories about how their giving is used to do God's work. And Foster has worked hard to help his congregation expand their understanding of generosity to go beyond what gets put in the offering plate. In the past, the church has gathered food for its food bank and collected clothing that it shipped back to Ghana, helping many members of the congregation maintain ties to their home countries.

It may sound as if Co-Heirs thrives as a generous church organically, but Foster admits that his church, like many, has challenges when it comes to living out this trait. Those challenges start with the makeup of the people in the pews. "Members are culturally, ethnically, and theological diverse, and though it poses some challenges among them," Foster says, "they have learned to hold on to their common identity and continue to discover new ways to embrace each other and also love all people as chosen by God." A generous church doesn't have to be homogeneous. God can work through, not in spite of, a congregation's diversity (whatever form it takes) to help a congregation thrive as it unites around a common call.

For Foster, that has meant helping his congregation overcome mindsets of scarcity, an understandable perspective for those who've fled their homelands to come to America. "My leadership style and culture of generosity are new to the members because of our cultural background," Foster says. "So, I have remained an example of what I represent, and [I] also encourage the congregation through education, training, and community projects." For a thriving congregation, generosity is a learned trait that must be continually practiced as a counter-cultural witness to our culture's call to hoard our resources for ourselves.

Despite his desire to model generosity for his congregation, Foster recognizes that, for Co-Heirs to thrive, he can't be the only one talking about what it means to be generous. So, he's found ways to invite the congregation to take the lead on nurturing a culture of generosity within the church. He says, "One of the Elders audited a stewardship course at Lexington Theological Seminary and impacted the congregation with his newfound perspectives. That supported our giving narrative."

Co-Heirs has come a long way since 2014, thanks in large part to Foster's steady leadership and visionary perspective. While the church's ten-year anniversary was an accomplishment to be celebrated, Foster sees it not as a finish line but as a starting point. "I'm not reflecting back, looking how far we've come. We are just going and going."

Foster's focus on helping Co-Heirs grow in their understanding of generosity is evident not only in their tangible actions but also in the perspective that motivates those actions. Emelia sums up that perspective when she says, simply but profoundly, "My understanding of generosity is kindness to all."

Second Christian Church, Mayfield, Kentucky

Generosity in churches can take many forms and stem from a variety of circumstances. For some churches, generosity is a characteristic ingrained in their DNA that continually reforms and regenerates as the church lives out its generosity in new ways. For other churches, like Co-Heirs, generosity is a trait that is learned as the congregation leaves behind negative connotations of the church's relationship with money and opens itself to the exciting things God is doing through it. And others…well, to paraphrase William Shakespeare, "Some are born generous, some achieve generosity, and some have the opportunity to be generous thrust upon them."

For Second Christian Church in Mayfield, Kentucky, the third way might best define how this congregation thrived in its generosity in the midst of the most tragic of circumstances. On the evening of Friday, December 10, 2021, an EF4-intensity tornado ripped through Western Kentucky, moving through eleven counties and causing fifty-seven deaths during its three-hour duration. One of the hardest hit areas was the small community of Mayfield (population around 10,000).

In Mayfield, homes were destroyed, cars were tossed around like toys, and a candle factory with 110 employees working inside was flattened. Three larger churches in downtown Mayfield sustained significant damage, including First Christian Church, whose domed roof and upper walls collapsed.

While Second Christian's building survived the tornado, it felt the pain of its community in the aftermath of the destruction acutely. Recognizing the immediate needs that surrounded them, the congregation sprang into action, responding to the call to live out their generosity in literally life-saving ways. "We were still in the cold and had no electricity, but we helped out as best we could," says pastor Antonio Sherrill.

In a matter of days, Second Christian was transformed from a church to a disaster relief command hub. The church became a distribution

74   THRIVING CHURCH

center, ensuring that much-needed supplies got into the hands of those most severely affected. Church and local community members, along with people from surrounding towns, came alongside Second Christian to help with the work. Week of Compassion, the Disciples of Christ disaster-response organization, provided generators so the church building would have heat and electricity. "We fed people and allowed our parking lots to be used by out-of-town and out-of-state groups who were coming in to serve the community," says Antonio.

But the support offered by Second Christian went beyond the tangible needs, tapping into the comfort and hope provided by faith. Ricky Winn, a long-time member of Second Christian, noted the outreach in response to the tornado, adds, "But most importantly, we were able to have prayer with everyone that came." Second Mayfield's response extended beyond the material to its spirit of care and concern for its community.

The church's generosity operated on both the macro- and micro-level. Along with the community-wide response, the church was blessed with funding that enabled it to help ten families that lost everything in the storms, offering them tangible help while also blanketing them in prayer. Countless people were given a sense of hope in the midst of the devastation because of Second Christian's generous response.

That's not a surprise to Antonio, who has called Second Christian home since he was three years old. As he grew, he bounced back and forth among several local churches until putting down roots at Second Mayfield in 2001. "When I arrived in 2001, the atmosphere of the church was saturated with the Holy Spirit," he says. "The presence of God has been in evidence ever since."

The presence of God's Spirit leading Second Christian goes all the way back to its founding in 1898. In its 126-year existence, the church has seen it all, from buildings on fire to tornadoes, and yet its witness continues to shine through the people who call it home. "I've seen many people come and go, many obstacles and hardships, a plethora of leaders," says Antonio. "But the atmosphere has always been welcoming, making us one family of God." While historically Second Christian's makeup has been African American, over the years it has attracted people from all walks of life and has expanded to include people of a variety of ethnic backgrounds.

The generosity which the church exhibited during the response to the tornadoes is indicative of the church's existence and its relationship with the Mayfield community. Because the congregation has been faithful in the little moments of generosity, it was able to respond faithfully when the community needed it the most. A thriving church doesn't just suddenly step up to address big needs: it is attentive to all the small ways in which its generosity can be put to use to serve God's kin-dom.

Second Christian does this in a variety of ways. "We have hosted community cookouts, offered free laundry for the community, allowed others to use our facilities and space, given financially to families and shelters, and built relationships with local nursing homes, meeting needs and having church services with them," says Antonio. Just when we thought Antonio had completed this already impressive list, he continues, "We have transported those who didn't have transportation, shared resources with those were in need, and assisted in other community outreach. Just two years ago we were recognized and received an award for our generous contributions to serving our community by Mayfield Minority Center."

What drives Second Christian's willingness to share its resources so abundantly? It starts with Antonio. "As the pastor, I have asked, 'What good is a ministry if it's not useful for the community it's located in?'" The question is refreshingly practical, yet it is grounded in a deeply theological belief that nothing we have is ours, but ultimately it belongs to God. Under Antonio's leadership, the people of Second Christian see themselves as stewards taking what they've been blessed with and using it to be a blessing to others. "We are seeking ways to please the Lord within and outside of our four walls."

Ricky also spoke about Antonio's leadership as being a catalyst to Second Christian's generosity. "Pastor [Antonio] Sherrill (who is also the principal of Mayfield Middle School) is hands-on in his teaching.

He doesn't mind getting his hands dirty. A common thread across thriving congregations is ministerial leaders who aren't afraid to lead by example, standing shoulder-to-shoulder with their congregation members as they serve.

The generosity of Second Christian has helped it thrive in making an impact in the Mayfield community, but Antonio isn't satisfied. "We are currently in the process of placing two big blessing boxes on our property for community needs to be met, as well as working with Week of Compassion and a community liaison to further meet the needs of our community. We have a vision of developing and building a life center to give life back in times of natural disasters, allow for the preparation of food and serving meal, as well as a bigger space for classes and events."

The 2021 tornado changed Mayfield forever. The recovery effort is far from over, and Second Christian continues to play a role. For example, it hosted a praise and worship concert on the two-year anniversary of the tornado, testifying to the town's resilience while remembering those that were lost. The community choir featured churches both local and out of town, and the concert made the TV news.

Redefining Generosity: It Doesn't Mean Big Budgets

The stories of Co-Heirs and Second Christian teach the church that generosity does not come only from financial resources. Generosity is positioning the church to see itself as caretakers of all that God has provided. Churches do not have to have an abundance of wealth in the membership of the congregation or in their budget in order to be generous. The generous church is one in which every gift is used for God's glory and God's work in the world. Generous congregations share what they have been given, no matter how small the gift may be.

Furthermore, the generous church has an outlook of gratitude. As the old hymn "Share His Love" says, "Because I have been given much, I too must give." For these churches, generosity is not only about money or "stuff." It is true that these churches will share their

Thriving Congregations Are Generous   77

financial and material resources when called upon to do so. But they also recognize that their very presence, their prayers, and their talents are gifts to be given away generously. They believe that generosity is one of the ways in which God's work is done in the world and that they are responsible for carrying God to their neighbors.

Churches that want to redefine generosity for themselves can begin by studying the scriptures about generosity. A useful tool for beginning that study can be found through the Center for Faith and Giving of the Christian Church (Disciples of Christ). The Center offers both a Study Document that was presented to the denomination's general assembly in 2017 and a curriculum based on the study document[3]. Centering generosity in the biblical texts enables members of the congregation to see themselves in the scripture and to learn how the ancient church understood itself as a caretaker and steward of all that God provides.

Cultivate a Culture

Generous churches excel at cultivating a culture of generosity in their members. Conversations around giving are not relegated only to "stewardship Sunday" but recur throughout the year. Giving, generosity, and sharing of resources are something that generous churches talk about as ways to fulfill their mission in the world.

Pastoral leaders cultivate a culture of generosity by modeling a generous life not just in the way they give of their funds, but also in how they spend their time, do their work, and care for the people who call the church home. Generous pastors work the fundraising booth at the downtown festival and help wrap gifts at the Christmas toy drive. Pastors who model generosity speak in board meetings about the multiplicity of ways the church has shared of itself in the community. They view their role as crafters of a vision of generosity. They report to the congregation regularly on the impact of its members' generosity.

When you ask a thriving generous congregation the question, "If this church ceased to exist in our neighborhood, who would miss

---

[3] You can find these resources and learn more at https://centerforfaithandgiving.org/.

us?" they know the answer. Lay leaders and "pew sitters" alike know that the blessing box and free library are frequented by the folks in the apartments a block over. They can tell stories of how the church showed up in a crisis. They recognize the church's contributions to the local school or nursing home. They know how the preschool which the church sponsors offers scholarships to families who cannot afford to send their children there. These congregations have fostered a culture in which talking about the good they do in the world through their generosity is not only normative but comfortable and expected.

At Co-Heirs, the culture of generosity stems from their lived experience as immigrants and refugees. Foster and the lay leaders use their stories to remind the people of the ways in which people were generous toward them when they arrived in the United States. They share about the welcoming spirit of a stranger, of resources provided by a church, of schools that willingly made accommodations for cultural differences. And the leaders translate that story into God being at work in their lives. God was fully meeting their needs when they were new to the United States, and so the church should strive to replicate that for others now.

Generosity Even When It's Tough

Natalie Sleeth's "Hymn of Promise" says, "In every bulb there is a flower, in the seed an apple tree." The promise of God is that the resources we have are sufficient. In a sinless world, there is enough food and water to sustain everyone on the planet. The earth produces and, if we tend it correctly, it will sustain us all.

But the systems are broken. The fulfillment of the promise of God that there is enough requires a partnership. From the very beginning of God's story in Genesis, God called the earth's people to be caretakers of the resources in partnership with God and the earth. God's kindom was created in such a way that we could share of ourselves, of our gifts, and of the fruits of the land and all would be fed and have their needs met. Greed has ruined the system. Instead of sharing and caretaking, we hoard God's resources and create scarcity for some while others allow things to go to waste. Scarcity is scary. Every church has known lean financial times that result from the broken system. Most churches have wrestled with their budgets, making difficult decisions to scale back or cut because of lack of resources.

What is the church to do when there "isn't enough?" Sometimes the resources of the people in the pews and even in the town or state are stretched so thin that the church is struggling to stay afloat. Sure, the church in the next county has a surplus of funds, but here…here there just is not enough to make ends meet.

Remember, generosity is not only about dollars. Second Christian could never have afforded to rebuild the homes people lost in the tornado. They did not have the financial resources to provide even one change of clothes to every person in need of them. For some churches, it would have seemed there was "nothing they could do." But not for a generous church like Second Christian. Second Christian said, "What *do* we have? We have square footage, and we have people who will pray." So they opened their doors and parking lot to the agencies with the financial resources to meet large scale recovery needs, and they began to pray.

Even when it seems there is no way your church can give, it can. It can give of its time, of its space, of its heart. The most generous churches may not have a single dollar to spare, but they have hearts that long to give, and they find ways to meet the needs in their communities.

Microphilanthropy and Stone Soup

Have you ever heard of the concept called "microphilanthropy?" It is a system of giving where everyone gives a very small gift—often $10 or less—and together it adds up to a significant total. The concept is rooted in the idea that when we all work together, we can do more. It is the origin of many denominations' missions and outreach efforts. "Every gift matters, no matter how small" is what you might hear from them. When Vermont Senator Bernie Sanders ran in the 2020 presidential election, he was known for citing the average donation of $27 to his campaign. His goal was to build the idea of microphilanthropy, to reassure you that even your $27 gift was enough to make a difference.

The story of Stone Soup comes to mind here. In the story, a town does not have enough food to feed themselves. A visitor to the town lights a fire in the middle of town and gets the biggest pot he can find. He begins to make soup, starting with only water and a few stones. When the townspeople become curious about what he is doing, he says, "I'm making soup." One by one, the townspeople bring something to add to the soup. One brings carrots, another celery, still another brings some seasonings, and on the story goes until a giant pot of delicious soup is simmering in the middle of the town. At the end of the story, everyone in the town feasts on the soup until they are sated.

What if the church could see its limited resources in the same way? Maybe you don't have anything beyond a few stones and some water. Maybe what you have is a great big pot. Maybe you grew an extra supply of carrots this year or your parsley is running amok in the garden. What do you have that your town needs? What can you contribute to the good work God is doing in the world where you live?

> *Generosity is a natural response to the abundance of God's blessings. From the time of Cain and Abel, God's people respond to God's blessings by bringing their offering as a gesture of gratitude. This offering takes many different forms, from crops to children to money. Regardless of the content, it's the meaning that is paramount. God blesses us and calls us to be a blessing.*
>
> *That's the message Paul is impressing on the Corinthians in his second letter to them when he writes, "And God is able to provide you with every blessing in abundance, so that by always having enough of everything, you may share abundantly in every good work" (9:8). God's abundance to us is not strictly for our own use, but for us to use in service to God's kin-dom. What we have is not ours. It is God's gift to us so that we may exercise the call to be generous.*

Texts for Study

- Genesis 2
- Deuteronomy 26:1–11
- II Chronicles 31:2–10
- Matthew 25: 31–45
- Luke 6:36–39
- II Corinthians 8:1–15
- Acts 4:32–37
- I Peter 4:10

QUESTIONS FOR DISCUSSION AND REFLECTION

1. Consider the story in Deuteronomy 26. What purpose does bringing the tithe serve in this story? How does your congregation celebrate the generosity of its members?

2. What biblical scriptures about generosity can you explore more fully in your congregation? How might you do this?

3. How does your church educate the congregation on generosity? What is the message you convey?

4. How might your congregation diminish its mentality of scarcity?

5. What are some specific examples of your congregation's current generosity?

6. What specific need can your church meet that is not currently being met?

7. What would it be like if your church were a community in which Acts 2 were lived out? How might it be possible for your church to model that?

Thriving Congregations Are Flexible

The Story of Wakonda Christian Church, Des Moines, Iowa

When you think of organizations that are flexible, we doubt churches would make the top ten. "Change" can sometimes be a four-letter word for a congregation, which seeks to hold fast to what is familiar in the midst of an ever-changing world. When everything else around them is constantly evolving, church members want their spiritual home to feel comfortable, steady…unchanging. And yet, the old axiom "change or die" has become an unfortunate reality for some churches who push back against the need to be flexible in the face of the constantly shifting sands around them.

Wakonda Christian Church in Des Moines, Iowa, has lived out flexibility as a trait from its earliest days. In 1960, just five years after it was founded, members of Wakonda traveled south to participate in the Mississippi Freedom Summer, a trip that transformed the pastor and members who attended, and ultimately the entire church. This fledgling congregation found a cause in the Civil Rights Movement and became a leading voice in the efforts to end redlining in the growing neighborhood around them. In 1965, the church established the Wakonda Preschool in an anti-racist effort to provide early childhood education to all children.

When the current pastor, Rev. Robyn Bles, arrived in 2018, the congregation was on the downhill slope of church growth. They had a large youth group but no children, and the writing was on the wall. The church was coming off two long pastorates (twenty-five and nine

84 THRIVING CHURCH

years, respectively) and, according to Robyn, was "eager for change and something new, while holding onto their Wakonda identity as a friendly, neighborhood church."

Conventional wisdom says that it takes a pastor a few years to truly establish themselves at a church and sufficiently earn the trust of the church members to be able to enact change and help the church move forward. For Robyn, that process was just getting started when the pandemic hit. COVID-19 was a catastrophic event, and many churches scrambled to figure out what it meant to be a church in such strained circumstances. Sanctuaries were empty. Offering slowed to a trickle. Committees and ministry teams stopped meeting.

Because of this, most churches became even less open to change, ironically in a time when churches needed to change even faster. But Wakonda was already poised to exercise flexibility in light of the world-changing circumstances. "We continued to be a congregation willing to try new things," says Robyn.

The groundwork for this attitude of flexibility was laid long before COVID. It started in the most sacred of church minefields: the sanctuary space. The design of Wakonda's sanctuary led to a pew layout that created a small dead space from which worshippers didn't have a direct line of sight to the chancel area. A TV was installed to improve visibility, but the space was still underutilized.

Robyn, whose spiritual DNA test showed she is 100 percent hospitality, dreamt of how that space might be used to minister to the littlest ones in the church. She re-envisioned the dead space in the sanctuary as a place for kids to be kids while their parents sat nearby. This area, cleverly named the "prayground," would be a safe space for kids to explore their spirituality at an appropriate level (or just get their wiggles out) while parents could worship just a few feet away.

But there was one small problem. At the time, the church really only had one little kid who would benefit from the "prayground." And it happened to be Robyn's daughter, Rosey. Still, the pews were already moveable, the church's preschool had extra toys, and the space was not being used in any meaningful way. So, the "prayground" was born.

Did everyone love the idea of the "prayground?" Not at all. Some people changed where they sat in the congregation to move away from the activity. And every once in a while, Robyn has to pause worship to ask the kids to "bring the noise down." Oh, but that all pastors had such a reason to pause worship, right? Being flexible means letting go of control, but the benefits brought by creative thinking are beyond what we can even imagine.

So how did Robyn cash in her relational capital to respond to these concerns? People have said, "You know, when I had kids, I either wanted them to go to the nursery or learn how to be in worship, which meant be quiet and sit still." While acknowledging that reality, Robyn helped the critics see that parenting has changed because the world has changed. Now, parents don't get as much time with their kids during the week as they would like, and most families want to be together as much as possible on Sunday mornings. "The prayground is not only allowing children to move the way children move, but it's allowing parents to engage worship more because they're not worried about keeping their kid entertained or about their kid disturbing someone else. Children and adults alike learn that making room for others is an act of worship."

In most churches, ideas about changes in the sanctuary can be the match that lights a stick of dynamite, but at Wakonda this change led to a different kind of explosion. "The prayground has grown so much that we had to take out an additional pew because we had so many children," says Robyn. Many of Wakonda's new young families cite the "prayground" as the reason why they chose to stay. One mother says, "A space was already prepared for me before I arrived." That's why Robyn says, "We are incredibly flexible because we are incredibly hospitable."

Robyn's boldness in asking her congregation to be flexible didn't stop there. Her next sanctuary sacred cow? The pulpit. Not the act of preaching, but the actual wooden structure in which she stood. It was designed by a previous pastor who took up much more space than Robyn, so when she stood in the pulpit, she couldn't see the first few rows of worshippers. The church already had a tradition of taking the pulpit down during the Advent season so as not to block the view of the giant Christmas tree. Robyn seized the opportunity to ask about taking it down full-time.

"Can you just get a stepstool?" one congregant asked.

"Have you watched me preach?" Robyn replied. "I'm gonna fall off that thing and break my ankle!"

So, the congregation went along with Robyn's idea, and their view—both literally and collectively—has changed.

If you're keeping score, that's two major changes to the sanctuary in Robyn's first few years at Wakonda. Such choices could be death sentences for some pastors, but Robyn's ability to read her congregation and her own intuition served her well in helping the church grow in its flexibility. "I've been very intentional about what I have asked to change," she says. And to this point, the congregation has yet to tell her "no."

Robyn attributes the congregation's flexibility to its thoughtful approach to change. "They're most willing to be flexible when they understand the changes being proposed, why they're trying this, and what the scope of change will be." Her intentionality and the pacing of change are hallmarks of her leadership and a big reason why the church goes down new roads with her. And Robyn is able to couch most changes in the language of "experiment," which gives some breathing room for those who might resist.

"I never make a hard and fast change," Robyn says. "I always put a timeframe on it and then (the congregation) is more willing to do it." When the change is marketed with "Let's give it a try," people are more inclined to see how it goes rather than oppose it from the beginning. And this creates dynamic space for people to generate their own ideas. "We had an older member join and she really wanted to do a Bingo night," Robyn says. "She was willing to organize it, so she did, and everyone was like, 'OK. We'll do this. We'll show up.'"

Why is Wakonda so flexible when most churches can become so institutionalized that any change, even a Bingo Night, is met with the tired retort, "We've never done that before"? Robyn's answer is funny and spot-on. "Midwesterners are ridiculously practical," she says. "If you explain it to them and say, 'Hey, we're gonna try this and this is why,' they're like, 'OK.'" You can't underestimate the power of good communication in helping a church be flexible. The more leadership can draw a map of where the church is heading—where the turns are, the potential potholes—the more likely the congregation is to go on the journey.

This trait served Wakonda well during the pandemic when, over a course of a few days almost all churches had to figure out how to be flexible. Thanks to Robyn's leadership, Wakonda was already there, and this allowed them to move beyond surviving to use the crisis to their advantage. For example, at a time when most churches were shutting down any future-focused processes, Wakonda was beginning to work on its vision as a church, even though the pandemic made the future much murkier. The congregation overhauled the leadership structure, rewrote the bylaws, and updated policies and procedures.

"I inherited a structure that was built for a 600-member, 300-worshipping community," says Robyn. Wakonda was no longer that size, but had retained the leadership structure, meaning that Robyn and the leaders of the church were dealing with a top-heavy model. Combine that with the pandemic, when no one was leading much of anything in the church, and the push to recruit was an uphill battle.

"We hunkered down and maintained everything for 2020," says Robyn. "So, for 2021 we were getting ready to do nominating, and I'm like, 'I'm not doing this.'" The congregation wasn't even worshipping together in their sanctuary, and yet people were about to be asked to step into leadership roles that no longer functioned and that no longer met the needs of the congregation. Once again, the Midwestern practicality won the day, and Robyn and her board leaders drafted some restructuring ideas and shared them with the congregation. "We hosted multiple Zoom town hall meetings. We sent letters. We sent emails. We were overly communicative, but I think people were also thirsty for information."

88   THRIVING CHURCH

Not everyone was on board with the change, but Robyn leaned into her, "Let's give it a try" approach to the transition process. "I said, 'We're giving ourselves three years to live into this because we're changing everything. If after three years we don't like this, we don't have to do it." Robyn acknowledged that "we don't know what we don't know" about the restructure, and gave the congregation space and grace to figure out if this new model would work for them. Not surprisingly, at the end of the three years, the church has fully lived into this new structure and is seeing the fruits of its efforts.

Robyn's approach to leading Wakonda models this willingness to embrace new ideas and directions. "I am a very flexible person, while understanding the balance of making thoughtful changes," she says. "I think my ability to work with my leaders in communicating the new idea while [also welcoming] their insight is tremendously helpful." Nancy Koll, a forty-five-year member of Wakonda, says, "Robyn shows flexibility in her daily being. She is always providing instructions to key people for how she envisions new and different approaches." Robyn is a team player, and the way in which she invites congregation members to participate in the leadership of the church opens them up to being flexible amid changing circumstances. "Collaboration and consensus building enables great trust, imagination, thus resulting in flexibility," she says. Robyn and Wakonda know that ministry is about partnership. This trust and knowledge gives the courage to be flexible and try new things.

Creative Thinking

Perhaps nothing is more foundational for congregational flexibility than creative thinking. Churches that want to be more flexible begin with problem-solving. Such churches look at their scenario, assess it, find the problems, and then wonder together how the problem might be solved in new, even unconventional, ways. When churches build the skills of thinking creatively, they are more likely to be flexible in urgent situations like the COVID-19 pandemic or when a hurricane or wildfire strikes. What Wakonda was able to do during the pandemic did not begin in the pandemic; it began early in Robyn's tenure when she implemented changes to the sanctuary.

Begin with Hospitality

Wakonda prides itself on being a hospitable congregation. Hospitality is deeper than welcoming; it attempts to imagine the needs outsiders might have and meet those needs before the newcomers arrive. Hospitality says more than "You are welcome here;" hospitality says, "We created this place with you in mind." Wakonda initially created the prayground in their sanctuary for one child—their pastor's young daughter. But they did not create the space to be suitable for only one child. If that had been their goal, they could simply have brought in one table and a couple of toys for her to enjoy during worship. Instead, they relocated a bookshelf, books, toys, building blocks, and several chairs and tables for children to use. They put some soft spaces on the floor for children who were still crawling. They anticipated that other families would want their children to be welcomed in that space. When other families began visiting the church, they found age-appropriate items in the prayground, regardless of the age of their children.

Churches can often accept changes better when they know the reason. If your congregation wants to make a change, perhaps the first question to ask is "Who benefits from this change?" More often than not, pastors and lay leaders want to make changes that make the church more open to people, more willing to meet needs, and more able to be in service to God and God's people. All of those things are rooted in hospitality. Even such changes as Wakonda made to its structure are rooted in hospitality: the church wanted to create a system that had busy and overstretched lay leaders at the forefront of their minds. They did not want to change their structure simply to make life easier on the pastor; they were looking to make the structure work for the congregation rather than the congregation work for the structure. Framing changes with this kind of hospitality helps the congregation strengthen its muscles of flexibility.

Over-Communicate Change

Flexible congregations know how to communicate within the church. It has often been said that you have to tell people at least

90 THRIVING CHURCH

three times before they hear you, and in an increasingly digital world, three times is likely not enough. Nowadays, churches have to think about who has heard the message, in what format the message was delivered, what was distracting people from hearing the message, and what other noises were competing with the message. Church leaders now have to imagine all of the ways in which people communicate with one another, and then interject themselves into those formats. You can make announcements from the pulpit, create a bulletin board, ask Sunday School teachers to discuss it, put it in the newsletter, and include it in your board report and still someone in leadership will say, "Why didn't I know this?"

It's helpful to remember how often you yourself have to see an advertisement before you begin to take notice of it. Some church leaders lose sight of how distracted church members are by their daily lives. Because pastors and lay leaders have been working on the prayground for months, it may feel like the information has been over-communicated to the congregation. In reality, any one individual member of your church may not have heard the message at all. If the newsletter didn't get opened and they are not on the board and their child was distracting them in worship on Sunday, they may have missed it.

Over-communicating with the church helps people feel more connected. When people know enough about an upcoming change to feel informed, they are more willing to trust the leaders guiding them on the journey.

Be Experimental

Wakonda's willingness to embrace the prayground and the new pulpit was largely successful because Robyn instituted an experimental period. For some congregations, pastoral authority is so high that the members will follow the pastor's leadership whether they agree or not. Their theology and polity claim that the pastor sets the vision for the church and the lay people are to support that vision in their work. For many congregations, though, the pastor has to persuade lay leaders to support the endeavor before the work can begin. In these cases, an experimental period of time gives the congregation agency to reject

Thriving Congregations Are Flexible 91

the dream of the pastor if it does not work out as the congregation had hoped. For example, if adding the prayground to the worship space meant that the congregation could no longer hear the sermon, they might have asked Robyn to reconsider the space. In return, Robyn could have offered to move the prayground to a different part of the sanctuary or to modify the audio system so that the activities of the children were less distracting. The experimental approach to change often results in congregations willing to try something new.

Some congregations are hesitant to experiment because they have been wounded by pastors and lay leaders in the past. In such cases, the congregation has trusted their leaders to guide them down a good path only to discover that the path is fraught with problems. One congregation we know had a new pastoral leader who wanted to use more contemporary music in worship. The congregation spent a hefty sum of money on new instruments and equipment for this musical change, only to find out the congregation did not know any of the songs and did not enjoy the music. The pastoral team pressed on, telling the congregation they would catch on to the music eventually. What resulted, though, was several members of the church no longer attending worship because they were frustrated by the musical choices forced upon them by their ministers.

Had that ministerial team been more intentional with the congregation, the music may have been met with different responses. What if the ministers had asked the choir to learn the music and lead in singing the songs? What if familiar songs had been played in a more contemporary way? What if the staff had tried an "experimental first Sunday of the month" worship service with instruments brought in by those who would play them? If the leaders had done more work in thinking creatively and implementing an experimental phase, the church might have been more flexible and agreeable with the change the pastors were trying to make.

Ask for Feedback

Asking a congregation for feedback demonstrates your own flexibility. Imagine you want to change the seating arrangement in your sanctuary. You would like to replace the hard wooden pews with individual chairs with padding on them. You follow all of the steps your leadership team has set up for listening to people in the congregation: you have listening sessions, you develop a budget you share with the congregation, you establish a window of time for experimentation, you explain the hospitality behind your desire to change the seating, and you ask them to trust you for three months. You remove four pews in different areas of the sanctuary and bring in forty padded chairs you have borrowed from another congregation. After the first month, you ask the people who have been sitting in those chairs if they like the change, and the resounding answer is that they hate them!

For many pastors this can feel like defeat. You asked the congregation to trust you, they went along with you, and they decided your way was wrong. But what if you didn't ask if they liked them. What if you asked how the chairs made the sanctuary feel different? What if you asked if the chairs made the people feel a different way during worship (not in their bodies, but in their minds and hearts)? And what if you asked them to return to sitting in the pews and then tell you again what they thought of the chairs? Perhaps it isn't the idea of chairs that is wrong, but that these particular chairs are uncomfortable. Or perhaps the pads on the chairs absorb too much sound and it is now harder to hear. Or perhaps the aisles are now too narrow for easy movement because the chairs are larger than the pews. By hearing the feedback of the congregation, you might discover that what appears to be the problem is, in fact, not the problem at all. Good questions elicit good feedback and better answers.

The most important part of seeking feedback is making sure it is taken seriously. If after asking the above questions your congregation says, "the pews were actually more comfortable and fit our worship style better," then the pastor does well to honor their willingness to try things with you. If you discover that the concept is working but the logistics of it are not, be flexible with the church; try something slightly different and ask for feedback again.

Nothing Is Permanent

"This is how we have always done it" is such a common mantra in churches that it could be etched into our communion tables. Congregations tend to forget that all ideas in the church were once new. Helping your church to see the changes you want to make as a "for now" change can help them to be more flexible. One congregation we know moved its communion table from the chancel to the floor to allow lay leaders who could not climb the chancel stairs to continue to serve at the table. Initially, some members of the congregation balked at the idea, saying they could not see as well as they had been able to see when the table was elevated. The pastor told the congregation that if the time came when all who wanted to serve at the table could climb the stairs, they would put the table back on the chancel. The congregation then understood the reason for moving the table as an act of hospitality and ministry. They also knew that the change in location of the table did not have to be a permanent change; if the time came when it could be on the chancel, the leaders were open to that option.

Helping your congregation see that nothing is permanent helps them to be more flexible in two ways. First, as we demonstrate above, it can help the church to experiment with you. Second, it helps them to understand that the things they see as permanent have in fact not always been so. As Erin once said to a church, "I doubt Jesus spoke into a microphone." Churches can name the ways their sanctuary and building have changed over the years; can they also name the ways their practices have changed? If not, perhaps learning some of those things will help them to be more flexible.

Let Go of Control

For pastors and lay leaders alike, control over a situation is difficult to relinquish. We all have our favorite ministries, beloved traditions, and golden calves—things in the life of the congregation we do not want to change. For congregations seeking to be more flexible, letting go of control can be the most difficult step to take. It is helpful for church leaders to remember that change is a vital part of all life, not just of congregational life. Living in a fast-paced world makes it even more

94 THRIVING CHURCH

difficult to let go of the control we have at our church—sometimes it seems like the only familiar place we have left.

Flexible congregations lean into a collaborative spirit to manage their needs for control. The church is better when we all work together for a common purpose. Letting go of control makes room for the Spirit to work among us, to blow the winds of change into our midst and provide fresh ways to be the church together.

> *Churches that are challenged by constantly changing circumstances can find solace in the stories of scripture, stories in which people were minding their own business when God rerouted their life plans. Noah's forecast was sunny skies until God told him to build a boat for a storm on the horizon (Gen. 6). Abram and Sarai were comfortable in Haran until God sent them a change of address (Gen. 12). Moses was happy herding sheep on Mt. Horeb until he turned aside to view a most peculiar shrub (Ex. 3). And the magi, after visiting the boy Jesus, were told to go home by another way to avoid Herod's wrath (Matt. 2). It's a good idea for God's people to stay on their toes, because we never know when God is going to call us to thrive in a new, unexpected way.*

Texts for Study

- Genesis 12:1–13:4
- Psalm 139
- Matthew 2:1–12
- Matthew 2:13–15

QUESTIONS FOR DISCUSSION AND REFLECTION

1. Consider Psalm 139. Why and how do you think this psalm speaks to flexibility in churches? What does it have to say God's leadership in your church?

2. Would you currently call your congregation a flexible congregation? If yes, how have you (or someone else)

fostered that? If no, how can you develop greater flexibility in your congregation?

3. What happens when your congregation encounters a problem? Who are the voices of influence in these difficult situations? How can these influential people foster a spirit of flexibility?

4. Name a time in your congregation's history in which you exhibited flexibility. What was significant about that experience for your church?

5. Often congregations who resist flexibility do so because they long to hang on to control. Of what does your church need to let go in order to be more hospitable?

6. Where would your congregation benefit from incorporating the "Let's give it a try" attitude of Wakonda?

Thriving Congregations
Are Willing to Take Risks

The Story of Midway Christian Church, Midway, Kentucky

Nestled in the heart of horse country amid the rolling fields of bluegrass, Midway, Kentucky feels like a throwback to a simpler time. Everything in the town is steeped in history. Midway, founded in 1833, features an historic district that was placed on the National Register of Historic Places in 1978. The Kentucky Female Orphan School was chartered in 1847 to educate orphaned girls and is now Midway University. And the town of just over 1,700 people is served by eleven different churches, many of them with deep roots in Midway's history.

Midway Christian Church (Disciples of Christ) is one of those churches, founded in 1844 when the town was still in its infancy. Now, 180 years later, the church resembles many Disciples of Christ churches in smaller towns around the state. The congregation is older, mostly retired, and exclusively white. It would be easy to conclude that Midway Christian is in the sunset period of its existence. It certainly wouldn't make most people's list of thriving congregations.

But Midway Christian is living proof that a church can be facing the typical challenges of small churches in America today and still do more than survive. Midway Christian is bucking the trend of declining churches, not just focusing on keeping the doors open but staying open to the movement of God's Spirit and boldly following her lead.

That Spirit is never one that calls us to complacency. We've yet to find that verse in the Bible where God calls someone and says, "You're

98 THRIVING CHURCH

doing great. Don't change a thing." Instead, God's call to God's people is one that involves staying on the move, being willing to change and innovate in order to put forward a relevant witness. That might be easy for a newer, younger church, but when you're 180 years old, the joints creak and the bones ache and sometimes all you want is a nap. And yet Midway Christian is awake and alert, taking risks that keep the congregation conversant with the needs of its community.

God's most recent invitation to Midway Christian to take risks started in 2006 when the church called Rev. Dr. Heather McColl to be its pastor. The previous minister had begun the process of helping the church ask, "What's next?" and had encouraged the church to consider a structure that would be more lay-led and less rigid. But that minister left before those conversations gained much traction. So, when she started, Heather notes, "The congregation was still very much minister-led, as had been the pattern since the beginning of remembered history, from what I gathered."

That was all about to change for the most beautiful of reasons. What better motivation for a congregation to take ownership of its own leadership than when the pastor announces she's pregnant? Midway Christian had called female pastors previously, but their children were either grown or they had chosen not to any. Therefore, the church had never needed a maternity policy. But now, a little child (or at least the promise of one) was going to lead them to take a risk in how they cared for their pastor and took responsibility for their ministry.

Heather recalls sitting in her office with the head of her Pastoral Relations Committee, a ninety-year-old retired executive. The last time he had stepped into a workplace, most of the women were secretaries and maternity leave didn't exist. Heather shared her good news and told the man that the church was going to need a maternity policy. To his credit, Heather said, the man was compassionate and supportive. But an important sea change had just happened, not just for the man, but for the entire congregation. Heather says, "I had just gone from being a minister, nondescript, wearing the black robe, standing behind the pulpit, to being a young woman with a life outside the church."

Perhaps for the first time, the good folks of Midway Christian Church were being forced to claim the title of the "priesthood of all believers," a risky proposition for a congregation that was used to the minister doing all the work. The governing board retired its rubber stamp, taking a more active role in the decisions that determined the mission of the church. The congregation became responsible for planning and leading worship on Sunday mornings. In essence, the church had to learn how to run itself from both a spiritual and practical standpoint. And as the congregation's members risked taking on these new roles, they grew in their faith and in their understanding of what it takes to run a church.

But they weren't the only ones. As Heather learned the new role of being a mom, she also developed a new understanding of her role as a minister. She says, "That time helped me realize that I was doing a disservice to the congregation by always taking care of everything, that I was not allowing them to be the full community of faith God had called them to be."

Upon her return after three months away, it was Heather's turn to take a risk. "As uncomfortable as it was for me," she says, "I let go of trying to manage everything and instead invited conversation and collaboration." That meant that some things didn't get done, a risky proposition for anyone who sits in the minister's office at a church. But Heather says that those moments led to "why" conversations, which let her reclaim her role as the minister of Midway Christian, "not the hired hand who dealt with broken toilets or mediated between contractors." That experience struck a new chord for the church and laid the groundwork for the congregation taking a much bigger risk just a few years later.

In 2010, Midway Christian participated in a regional initiative that encouraged congregations to live more fully into a missional ministry mindset. For Midway Christian, that meant being challenged to become more engaged with its community. In answering this challenge, the church discovered an urgent need hidden beneath the small town's charming, affluent veneer: a high rate of food insecurity. The congregation discovered it was situated in a partial food desert,

100 THRIVING CHURCH

with only one grocery store that carried limited fresh produce and had comparatively higher prices.

Exacerbating the issue was the lack of public transportation to adjacent communities with more grocery options. A neighboring town had resources to address food insecurity, but many of the residents who would benefit from those services didn't have a way to get to them. The regional initiative had worked in that it encouraged the church to be more missional. Now that the mission was identified, how could the church help to meet the need?

A member of the congregation who is also a successful local chef had the solution: the church could get its kitchen certified by the health department. This would accomplish two goals, according to Heather. "This would allow us to rent it out to local producers, providing income for the church while supporting our Green Chalice initiative. It would also allow us to serve a monthly free community dinner as a way to help address food insecurity within our Midway community." Turning a treasured sacred space like a church kitchen into a community shared space...what could go wrong?

Well, nothing. At first. The congregation embraced the idea, setting aside several days for painting, cleaning, and organizing. Heather said, "Everything was going great—until it came to dealing with the old church softball trophies, gathering dust and grease on the top shelf."

Ah, the old softball trophies. Every church has them, right? If not a trophy, then a gaudy, thread-bare tapestry or a rusted plaque or a donated picture of a white, angelically coiffed Jesus. Every church has some touchstone to the past that "no one" wants to mess with because "someone" might get upset. These items function as a historical talisman, imbued with almost magical significance, and can often be both symbolic and real-life roadblocks to a church moving forward. Sometimes, the biggest risk a church can take is to leave behind its past in order to embrace the future God has ordained for it.

That's the risk Midway Christian faced when the health department said the softball trophies had to go. Heather recalls,

"I kept hearing over and over, 'We can't get rid of these! They are from when we won the softball tournaments!' I admit I...not very pastorally asked, 'If they are so important, why are they in the kitchen gathering dust?'" While the question may not be pastoral, it's pointed for all the right reasons, holding up a mirror to Midway Christian's desire to stay who they were instead of taking the risk to become who they might be for the benefit of their community.

No one could answer Heather's question, so the church kept a couple of the trophies to be placed in the church's "Hall of History," and the rest were offered to the people who had been on those winning teams. Turns out, they didn't want the trophies, either! With the glove-wielding idols gone, the church could move forward with the vision of making a real difference in helping to feed the most vulnerable in their community.

Of the trophies, Heather says, "This clinging to what was in hopes that someone would pick it up someday almost derailed the vision of what has become one of Midway Christian's most successful ministry opportunities—our monthly free community dinner in which we feed over 100 meals to individuals and families in Midway and surrounding areas in Woodford County." Thriving congregations find that on the other side of the risk that needs to be taken can be blessings that are multiplied exponentially for the sake of God's kin-dom.

Those dinners have been transformative for the church and the community. Church member Adele Dickerson says, "Those who attend express their appreciation, not only for the food, but for the opportunity it provides to visit with people in the community and build relationships." The risk the church took to turn its facilities outward to the community has been a blessing to those being served and those who are serving. Now that's an effort worthy of a trophy!

Community engagement of this sort continues to be a hallmark of Midway Christian's identity. Church member Sandy Gruzesky says, "As a church, we have prioritized engaging with the community (local, regional and global) from a variety of perspectives. We have found this to be the most authentic way for us to live the gospel of Christ and

102 THRIVING CHURCH

give it relevance in the world we live in today." Sandy cites examples like live-streaming worship, pursuing ecumenical opportunities, and a focus on fairness and social justice issues as evidence of Midway Christian's growing witness.

Sandy calls this move to take ministry outside the walls of the church's building an "active risk." She says, "Active risk opens our hearts and minds to clearly see opportunities to shine the light of Christ, opportunities that we may not have otherwise seen." To fail to take an active risk is in itself a risk—"the risk of becoming irrelevant in a world full of injustices," Sandy says.

The change in congregational identity that started with a birth announcement and took shape in a transformed church kitchen continues to bear fruit for Heather and the congregation. While the pastor/laity role is still a work in progress, which is common for every congregation, the pastor's and laity's willingness to trust each other makes taking risks less frightening. Heather says, "At a recent leadership retreat, I started the conversation about not being able to do everything, while still visioning for our community of faith. The life-giving thing was [that] the leadership recognized this, as well." That has led to the church budgeting for support staff to free up creative space for Heather to dream about Midway Christian's future.

Heather's courage to take a risk in her conversation with church leaders is a model for her congregation on the importance of not staying safe. When it comes to the church's boldness, Heather is, in the words of Sandy, "the initiator and instigator"— which she says with much admiration. Sandy adds that Heather's willingness to address controversial topics in her sermons has made the church more courageous in tackling difficult topics and engaging in "deliberative dialogue." Dickerson agrees, adding, "She leads us in discussions that are challenging and designed to expand our knowledge and beliefs."

To continue to be a thriving congregation, Midway Christian is committed to staying focused on who God is calling them to be. "We don't define our success in the same terms as defined by the world," says Sandy. "Rather, we are focused on shining the light of Christ." To

Thriving Congregations Are Willing to Take Risks   103

keep shining that light, the church realizes it needs to continue taking risks and being willing to innovate. And it is. The church's areas of focus for the coming year include racial reconciliation, creation care and how it impacts the church, and connecting to the community locally and digitally.

Digitally? Pretty risky for a 180-year-old. But also necessary to continue thriving.

The Risky Church

"Taking a risk" may seem foolish to those of us who cherish our safety and security. We don't climb mountains or hang glide off cliffs. We're reticent to let our gas gauge fall below a quarter of a tank. We'll even think twice before eating two-day-old leftovers. But for churches, risk-taking can be both more mundane and crucial for survival (but no less scary).

Thriving congregations recognize that risks are a part of the journey of growth. While complacency may be more comforting, it can lead to stagnation, and before a church realizes, it has become a museum, a monument to what used to be rather than a road sign of where God is calling it. What does risk-taking look like in a thriving congregation?

Innovation as a Component of Risk-Taking

A key component of being willing to take risks is innovation. Innovation involves three key characteristics: new thinking, new actions, and increased value. Continuing to use old ways of thinking will only produce the same tired ideas. For example, what if instead of basing your fellowship meal schedule on the traditional calendar (an Easter meal, a summer picnic, and a holiday meal in the winter), your congregation thought about fellowship meals based on the school calendar? Could fellowship meals be a way to celebrate kids and young adults returning to school each semester and then a meal for celebrating your graduates? What would that do to the way your church thinks about meals and time together? Perhaps this new way

104   THRIVING CHURCH

of thinking about meals would produce new actions; maybe the meal is more tailored to kids and families and less traditional. What would that change do to your congregation's value of the educators and kids and young adults in your congregation? Would it add value to fellowship among your young families?

Supportive Relationships

Congregations that thrive in risk-taking have to work in relationships. The relationships between pastor and formal lay leaders (board chairs, officers, trustees, and others) must already be strong before a congregation is willing to take a risk. When a key number of congregational leaders see the value in the risk, the congregation follows suit. In every congregation, the key number is different. For an older congregation like Midway Christian, it may take just a few key stakeholders to shift the tide. For a suburban congregation with a large attendance and regularly changing faces, it may take as many as half of the attendees to create congregational support for taking a risk. Determining who those key players are in the congregation is the first step to developing the willingness to take risks.

Congregations who are not yet risk-taking congregations can begin by developing these relationships of trust between the pastor and the most prominent lay leaders in the congregation. That may take the form of meetings to talk about the future of the church or sharing coffee time to chat about your favorite sports team for a while before turning the conversation to the church. Our experience with thriving churches tells us that all congregations take small risks regularly, but risk-taking congregations have developed the skills to accept risk.

Every congregation has to do risky things at times. Maybe the budget needed is higher than the pledges received, but the church moves forward because it believes in the work the budget supports. Embarking on a year in which you do not know if you can pay all of the bills or not is a risk that many congregations take annually. The bigger risks of a risk-taking congregation are those that move the church forward in its mission. Midway Christian took the risk of remodeling the kitchen (and the expenses that involved) because doing so aligned closely with the church's value of feeding the hungry.

We suggest three steps to build these relationships:

Move at the Speed of Trust. In his book of the same title, Steven Covey uses the phrase "the speed of trust" to talk about how organizations build relationships within the system. Some churches are resistant to risk because of their past history. They've been mistreated by pastors, or a church split has squelched their energy. Some churches are resistant because they're living with a scarcity mindset, which will be discussed later in this book. Other churches have strong ties within and among the laity and feel as if the pastor is an interloper in their business; this happens most often in congregations with a history of short pastoral tenures. The pastor has to develop relationships at the pace of the laity and not expect the laity to trust the pastor simply because of the office. Find out as much as you can about the church's history. Discover what it means to have been a lifelong member of this church. Explore how these particular leaders have been shaped by their relationship to the church. All of this research and homework should be done before you begin trying to foster deeper relationships with the lay leaders. Carry that information with you as you bond.

Gather Intentional Groups. A congregation in a parallel Lilly Project grew deep connections among the men in the congregation when the pastor started inviting one or two guys over to his house on Friday nights for a bonfire. They'd spend the evening hanging out in the pastor's backyard: sometimes grilling, sometimes playing yard games, sometimes talking sports, sometimes something more meaningful. Over time, these opportunities to get to know one another grew into conversations about the men's spiritual lives, about their struggles to find their place in the congregation, and the stresses they brought into the room. These social events gave the pastor time to get to know the men of the congregation on more than one level of intimacy. From these relationships, fresh ideas for the congregation's ministry developed. These men became the support system the pastor needed to help move the congregation forward in taking risks.

106   THRIVING CHURCH

Start with Necessity. In the case of Midway Christian, Heather's impending maternity leave forced the congregation to think about their view of the pastoral role. Not every congregation has that luxury. Often, congregations are not "forced" to have to change anything. Allowing trust to develop over time helps the congregation see how their mission and values require some changes and prepares them for the moment when risk-taking is not a choice but a requirement for continued thriving.

Reframe Failure...and Try Again!

You don't have to lead your congregation to take major risks the first time through. One congregation we've studied was recently changing its governing documents. Some of the leaders in the congregation wanted to change the expectations of the deacons, giving them more responsibility and modifying who was eligible to serve. During the process of receiving feedback from the congregation, the church made it abundantly clear that they were not ready to release their long-held traditions around deacons. The leadership proposed a middle-ground to the congregation that was then widely accepted. The leadership team could have seen this as a failure—for not moving the congregation away from their traditionally-held views on deacons. However, the team instead chose to see all the ways the new governing documents moved the congregation toward a deeper sense of their values and priorities, while keeping this element of their history. The leaders chose to see the big picture and celebrated the risks the congregation *did* choose to take, refusing to see the rejected changes to the deaconate as a failure.

Some congregations have spent an entire generation with pain or scarcity. It may be that they simply aren't ready to adopt changes they see as too risky. That's OK. The journey toward taking risks is precisely that: a journey. If the path you take leads you to a dead end, just circle back and try again. If you feel the congregation trusts you as the pastor and also trusts the lay leaders, then maybe the one risk you want them to take is too big. If that's the case, then perhaps a smaller step forward is in order currently. The more you accomplish together, the more willing the congregation will be to risk something bigger.

Ask Good Questions

When Midway Christian set out to remodel the kitchen, the church began with a critical question: What is missing in our community that we are uniquely gifted to provide? This question led the way as the church moved forward to feed its neighbors experiencing food insecurity. They found in themselves a giftedness and a passion they could channel into a desperately needed service for their community.

But, the trophies. That the health department mandated that the trophies had to go surely helped the congregation embrace the change. It wasn't just that Heather thought they looked unsightly; they were a hazard to public health and an obstacle to the church's new missional mindset. Yet the congregation still wanted to keep them because someone might be upset.

Someone, who we vaguely assume exists, is the most dangerous person in every congregation. Someone holds significantly more power than any congregation should give them. Someone can be code for "I know who, but I don't want to say," or it may literally mean "there might be a person." Sometimes it's the fear of what could happen that keeps churches from taking risks, even if that threat never actually materializes.

Part of moving forward when that someone shows up is figuring out which type of someone is in the room. Is it the "I know who, but I don't want to say?" That someone should never have a place in a church. That someone creates triangulation and secrecy—the enemies of trust. If there is a person who says "Someone," but won't specifically name the person, it's important for the congregation's leaders to address

108   THRIVING CHURCH

this behavior. That someone either needs to be named so the problem can be handled well, or that someone ought not to be present in the conversation.

If, however, the someone who shows up in the meeting is actually an assumption of a someone who may be there, this is much easier to address. Here, we return to listening. Ask a long-time member to tell you the story behind the fear caused by changing this item or policy or system. Ask and ask until you find the answer. In the case of the trophies, the church discovered that even those who played on the teams did not want the trophies. The someone in the room turned out to be no one. The congregation at Midway Christian found a compromise by placing a few trophies in their "Hall of History" alongside other memorabilia that tells the church's story, but that someone was no longer allowed the power to control the church's mission.

Celebrate the Rewards

When congregations do the work of listening well to one another, building trust, and engaging in intentional work around their calling, they can be the risk-taking congregation they are called to be. As believers in the God who calls people to take risks throughout the scriptures, the risk-taking church more fully lives into God's dream for the world.

When the risk taken proves to be vital to the overall wellbeing of their community, leaders should celebrate that work. The pastor and the lay leaders need to remind the congregation of the good work they did in making a change, taking a risk, and reaping the reward of a job well done. When the congregation can see the benefit, their risk has brought about, then they're ready to take their next step forward. The more a congregation takes risks and sees the success, the more willing they are to consider risking again. The work of the leaders in these congregations is to celebrate the rewards, honor the process, and prepare the church to do it again. Congregations who take a risk and move forward to where God has called them often find that God will call them again to take another step into the unknown. Their work is only beginning!

> *God's call to God's people always involves risk. We do not follow a God of comfort and complacency, but instead pledge our allegiance to a God who loves us for who we are but knows we are capable of so much more. In the Bible, God calls a bumbling, stuttering Moses to stand up to the most powerful man in the world in order to free God's people from four hundred years of slavery in Egypt. Jesus calls an impulsive Peter to take the risk of leaving the safety of the boat to experience the thrill of walking on water and of radical trust in Jesus. And the Holy Spirit calls Phillip to the wilderness to witness to a non-Jew, the Ethiopian eunuch, in order to give God's word a wider audience. These three examples, and so many more throughout the Bible, demonstrate that God's call comes with a risk, requiring trust in God's promises to move forward in faith.*

Scriptures to Study

- Exodus 3:1–4:17
- I Samuel 3:1–21
- Jonah 1:1–17
- Matthew 4:18–22
- Acts 8:26–40

QUESTIONS FOR DISCUSSION AND REFLECTION

1. What is the riskiest thing your congregation has done in the past year? What did you learn from that action?

2. Think of an instance in which your congregation took a risk that did not end well. If you were to take the same risk now, how would you plan for it differently? What steps would you take to encourage your congregation to ask, "Why not?" about that situation.

3. Which scripture (perhaps among those listed above) most resonates with you about taking risks? What is it about that story that is particularly meaningful to you?

110 THRIVING CHURCH

4. What prevents your congregation from being willing to take risks right now? How can you build members' confidence to try new things?

5. What recent successes can you point to that build your congregation's confidence?

Thriving Congregations Are Forward Thinking

The Story of New Century Fellowship Christian Church, Louisville, Kentucky

It seemed somewhat fitting that when we contacted Rev. Dr. Syvoskia Pope to talk about her church, New Century Fellowship Christian Church, she was delayed in responding because the church was moving to a new location in the Shively neighborhood of Louisville, Kentucky. Of course it was. The folks at New Century Fellowship have been moving since it was founded in 2013, always going to where God is calling them to go next.

The seeds for that forward-thinking spirit were planted by Syvoskia back in 2012 when the Kentucky region of the Christian Church (Disciples of Christ) granted her a license for ministry. That was like opening the starting gate at the Kentucky Derby, because Syvoskia took that license as permission to truly dream about God's future for her. While she was serving another church, she said, "Through my own spiritual practice, fasting, and prayer, the Lord gave me the name 'New Century Fellowship.'"

Armed with only a name and a call (which is more than enough for God to work with), Syvoskia informed the seminary where she was taking classes and the commission that was overseeing her journey in ministry that God had called her to start a church. What else could they say but, "Yes!" Syvoskia recalls. "I guess they looked at me and said, 'She sounds like a woman who has made up her mind!'" Syvoskia is proof that God's call doesn't require you to be fully equipped. Like Moses, like Abraham, like Mary, she heard God's call and said, "Here I am," trusting that God would provide what was needed for the journey forward.

112   THRIVING CHURCH

In 2013, New Century Fellowship was incorporated as a nonprofit organization and began hosting monthly worship services for youth and young adults in a small event hall that was part of a radio station. In the beginning, the members of the congregation were mostly under forty and predominantly African American. In 2014, New Century Fellowship was officially launched as a new church start in the Region of Kentucky.

Syvoskia's vision for the church was expansive, meaning that the congregation might not look like other churches around it. For example, Syvoskia started a Monday night service located in a group of three halfway houses. "I think we picked up about twenty ladies that were there," Syvoskia says. "They're getting their salvation and we're baptizing them in the backyard of the houses." New Century Fellowship led services for the women every Monday, and it wasn't unusual for some of the women to attend Sunday morning worship at the church, as well. "I can remember a time at Christmas where we had them all in robes and in the choir because we needed extra people to sing," Syvoskia says. "We just had so much fun loving on them." Even in its infancy, New Century Fellowship was less concerned about its own survival than it was about sharing the gospel in forward-thinking ways.

One of the characteristics of New Century Fellowship that keeps them looking forward is that there is no past that holds them down. When you start a new church, the slate is blank, which unmoors you from the anchors of the past that can prevent you from moving full steam ahead into God's future. When New Century Fellowship started, the congregation was ready and eager to do ministry, to discover where God was calling it to go. Pope says, "We had much zeal for the Lord. We were ready to serve and conquer it all."

The lack of a past has been a catalyst for the congregation at New Century Fellowship as it writes its own story. "We are definitely risk-takers on this journey," says Pope. Whereas more established congregations might have more to lose by looking forward, New Century Fellowship can do so unencumbered. Pope says, "We often say, 'Why not?' We have never done it before, so what can be the worst

Thriving Congregations Are Forward Thinking   113

thing to happen?" This lack of fear of failure is a crucial component of being a forward-thinking church.

Syvoskia's zeal for the Lord and this new church was infectious to those around her. For example, Dr. Mary Simmons had worked with Syvoskia for several months without knowing she was a pastor. Mary was herself a follower of Christ, but due to some previous hurts had no interest in setting foot in a church again. Syvoskia saw a light in Mary and wasn't afraid to call it out. "She approached me and stated I need to get to somebody's church because I had too much power inside of me," says Mary. So, Mary started visiting churches, still not aware of New Century Fellowship and Syvoskia's leadership role in it.

One day, Mary arrived late for an important meeting and Syvoskia told Mary she was in no condition to participate. Mary feared a reprimand, so imagine her response when Syvoskia asked if she could pray for her! Mary says about that prayer, "I had never experienced such a warm sensation that swept over me, that regulated my mind and comforted my soul." Mary asked where Syvoskia attended church and has been a member of New Century Fellowship ever since.

Mary sings the praises of Syvoskia's leadership. "Pastor is a strategic visionary," Mary says. "Envisioning anything requires boldness, courage, and being a forward thinker. Pastor is the epitome of this." Syvoskia sees her church members as potential leaders who will help usher the church into the future God has ordained for it. "Pastor began to disciple and develop our character, cultivate our talents, and leverage our gifts," says Mary, who talks about attending "Pastor's Master Class," a Sunday meal with Syvoskia where Mary learned about growth and the development of her character for leadership. A thriving congregation and the pastors who lead it see its members as an integral part of capturing the vision and looking forward and help them develop those gifts.

For New Century Fellowship, that forward-thinking mentality led the church to be on the move—literally— as it followed God's leading. Syvoskia tells the story of driving by a UCC church in 2015, a church located about three miles from the radio station, and of turning her head and hearing the Spirit say, "Well that's gonna be your church." She wrote a letter to the pastor and slipped it under the church door, and forty-eight hours later received a call from the pastor asking for a meeting.

Not long after that, New Century Fellowship moved to the UCC church, a group of people that, in many ways, could not have been more different than them. When Pope and her people moved in with the existing congregation, it was more of a transactional relationship, but Syvoskia and the UCC pastor were looking forward to more.

The UCC pastor left before that relationship could develop and the UCC church found itself without a leader. They contracted Syvoskia to do pastoral care, and she eventually took on a larger role in the church. But in the midst of talks of a potential collaborative partnership, with Syvoskia slated to be the pastor of both churches, the lay leadership of the UCC church abruptly decided to close its doors and sell the building. It turns out this graying, white congregation had difficulty adapting to a worship style to which they were not accustomed, and eventually, in Syvoskia's words, "they ran out of steam." The UCC church's decision meant that New Century Fellowship was going to be—you guessed it—on the move again. But this time the church had only three weeks to find a new location.

Most churches would have panicked, but not New Century Fellowship. Syvoskia's visionary leadership had conditioned the members to keep their eyes looking forward. Even in the midst of difficult and unexpected circumstances, forward-thinking congregations turn crises into opportunities to witness to the provision and presence of God. "Obviously, we finished what we needed to do there," says Syvoskia. "Now God is calling us to new territory, so let's bring our spirit there." Thanks to Pope's steady hand and the congregation's willingness to keep looking ahead, the question "What's next?" was an exciting rather than a daunting one.

The church's willingness to ask that question over and over again fueled the creation of the most powerful example of New Century Fellowship's thriving (and there are many). It would be understandable for a new church start to turn its focus inward, channeling its resources to help support the establishment of the institution. But, as we saw with the worship services at the halfway houses, New Century Fellowship doesn't exist to serve itself, and a big part of its thriving is how the church has engaged with the needs of the community.

Founded in 2017, the Empower Hope Center exists to help the church build partnerships with the community in ways that make a tangible difference for those connected to the Center. The Center works with Boy Scouts, seniors, the Urban League, the Metro United Way, and many more non-profit organizations to serve the Louisville community. While it was started as a church outreach, the center was so successful that it now has its own board and is a separate 501(c)3 entity from the church.

Pope says, "The Empower Hope Center model gives the opportunity to create partnerships locally and beyond to serve the community." The Center has celebrated success through workforce development in job training and promotion of people seeking employment, helping them overcome personal challenges that have kept them from finding a job. "We train them with mock interviews, teach them how to put a résumé together, and really help them understand the paradigm," says Syvoskia.

The Center has also trained laity and other church leaders, using a curriculum written by Syvoskia. The Center has also focused on families, helping them navigate through financial wellness and preparing them for home ownership. And Syvoskia says the Boy Scouts are akin to the church's youth group, and that the Center is planning a youth entrepreneurial leadership program for the Scouts in the coming year.

Because of successes like the Empower Hope Center, New Century Fellowship has made an impact that is exemplary for a church of its age and size. "We are a church that goes outside its walls," says member, Dr. Ciceley "CC" Bishop. "We seek what the needs of the community are and do our best to be a resource." If the church were to close its doors tomorrow, it would have accomplished more than many congregations that have been around ten times longer than

116   THRIVING CHURCH

it has. But Pope, a creative thinker, has no plans for New Century Fellowship to slow down.

In fact, the church just celebrated its tenth birthday by receiving its official charter as an established congregation from the Kentucky region of the Christian Church (Disciples of Christ). Syvoskia said this was a significant milestone because it showed her congregation what they were capable of accomplishing in Christ's name. "I told them, 'You keep looking at me like it's my church. This charter says that it's our church.'" New Century Fellowship has done what most new church starts don't. Despite the challenges, the obstacles, and the moves, they've made it.

But this is not the end of the story for New Church Fellowship: it's just the starting point. This is no time to rest. Syvoskia already has big plans for the congregation moving forward. When I ask her "What's next?," she talks about women empowerment and marriage groups, and about renewing their commitment to fellowship with each other. Then, she pauses and says, "I have contacts in Africa. I'm dreaming about New Century Fellowship Global." Of course she is. That's what forward-thinking leaders do: they dream big and let God illuminate the way.

Always Be Moving

Unlike New Century Fellowship, your church does not have to move physical locations to be a church on the move. Churches are on the move when they are listening to the Spirit and dreaming about what God has in store for them. Complacency is not an attribute of a forward-thinking church. As Syvoskia says, "What's next?"

The COVID-19 pandemic reminded churches that the future is uncertain. Five-year plans seemed irrelevant in the face of an uncertain tomorrow. That sense of uncertainty kept even some of the most vibrant congregations stalled for quite some time. And yet, churches like New Century Fellowship saw the pandemic as a new opportunity for ministry. Across the United States, churches stepped up to handle the immediate crisis, serving as testing sites and vaccine education centers for the local community.

Even more striking than meeting the immediate need, churches like New Century Fellowship saw the pandemic as a reminder that God has always been at work in the life of the church, especially in difficult times. When the road ahead is treacherous, our tendency is to slow our pace, walk more carefully, and avoid any risky behaviors. But forward-thinking congregations have the unique ability to say, "This is brand new territory. Let's explore how God might be at work here."

Untether from the Past

Congregations with a long history may look at the story of New Century Fellowship and think, "It's easy for them; they don't have a history that binds them to traditions." But that is not true. Even the youngest congregations have patterns and systems they follow. What makes New Century Fellowship different is that their history and systems are not what define them; they allow their story to inform what they do, but they do not let the story hold them in place.

Releasing our past is a challenge for most congregations. Whether the church is a few years old or centuries old, people will look to the church's traditions as an anchor. Memory ties us to "the good times" when the sea gets rough. What forward-thinking congregations do that is different is to use "the good times" as a reminder of God's faithfulness. They look back at those good times and are reminded that just as God held them steady then, so too God will hold them steady now. The past is not a place to which to return, but a marker of God's faithful provision.

Historical congregations in particular are prone to anchor themselves in the past. Churches founded over a hundred years ago pride themselves on their resilience and their tenacity to get through the worst events in their history. Such churches often give the major events that shaped their church nicknames: The Fire. Segregation. The Financial Crisis. The Murder. That One Pastor. The Church Split. They often remember these events as difficult times that should be a warning to the church. Forward-thinking congregations see such events differently: they see them as times when God was faithfully leading them through something difficult. They are stories of God's presence in crisis as a demonstration that God will be faithful again. To untether the church from the past is not to dishonor the past; rather, it is to learn from the past and to use what the church learns to look for what God is doing next.

Don't Wait for Permission

Forward-thinking churches see crises as opportunities. In the case of New Century Fellowship, when the UCC church decided to close and sell their property, the leaders saw it as a message from God: "Our work here must be finished; let's see where God is sending us next." They did not need to wrestle with the loss of the space because they see themselves as a church on the move. New Century Fellowship aims to meet the needs around them; however, God calls them to do that. To them, a change in plans means God must be ready to do something new.

Depending on your denominational structure, waiting for permission may be a more complicated component of being a forward-thinking congregation. Some traditions are bound by practices and governance that slow down the work of the local congregation. In such scenarios, we recommend congregations develop a mentality of "when they say yes" instead of "if they say yes." Plan and work toward your goal, presuming that your leaders are going to allow you to follow your dream. You might have to wait for permission to act, but no church has to wait for permission to dream!

Train Up Good Leadership

A thriving congregation and the pastors who lead it see its members as an integral part of capturing the vision, looking forward, and helping them to develop those gifts. Syvoskia is a team builder by nature. She knows how to surround herself with people who have gifts for leadership. She sees how the work they do professionally can serve the wider church, even when it seems unrelated to ministry. She does not hesitate to tell them that God is at work in their lives. Strong pastors with vision for the future practice the skill of identifying a call.

Syvoskia then trains and mentors these leaders to use their gifts for ministry. She meets people in their particular place of giftedness and helps them to find a way forward. The pastor who can surround herself with good leaders and then trust them to do their work has more bandwidth for dreaming. One member at New Century Fellowship is a certified Workforce Development Trainer, and another member is a Certified in Youth Development. Part of what Syvoskia and New Century Fellowship do so well is to use people in lead in ways they are already gifted to do. The leaders of New Century Fellowship design ministry programs around the knowledge and skills of their laity. In the future, that may mean that Youth Development is not a project New Century Fellowship does; but we are certain that whatever the church does, it will continue to help its skilled laity to use their gifts for God's good work in their part of the world.

Empower Hope

New Century Fellowship's 501(c)3, The Empower Hope Center, is the driving ministry of the congregation. The church's mission is to prepare disciples for ministry...and to build up the Kingdom of God throughout the world. The Empower Hope Center is how they live that out. Your church may not need a separate nonprofit to do the work you are called to do, but what New Century teaches us is to weave our work so innately into our mission that the outside world cannot see a difference between who we are and what we do.

The mission of the Empower Hope Center is to empower families, to change lives, and to bring transformation in the community. The Center seeks to offer a broad range of social programs that meet practical needs in the lives of people who cross the threshold. The Empower Hope Center's purpose is to help build job skills, prepare teens for their future, support single moms, and so much more. While New Century Fellowship is not yet able to meet all of the needs it claims in its vision, precisely that is what makes it such a forward-thinking congregation: it has a vision for what the future can hold. New Century Fellowship and the Empower Hope Center are

120   THRIVING CHURCH

unwilling to be satisfied only by what they can do right now. They are dreaming of ways in which they can use the skills they already have in the congregation to create better lives for people in their communities. They offer hope to their neighbors and to themselves by dreaming of a future that meets the needs of people around them.

Think Beyond Now

Few mainline congregations in the United States now are dreaming about planting branches of their ministry overseas. New Century Fellowship is. Its visionary work and desire to meet people's needs leads them to think constantly about what may be in their future. Syvoskia dreams of a day when God allows New Century Fellowship to found a church on the continent of Africa. She dreams of an Empower Hope Center that can meet the needs of every person it encounters. She looks forward to the day when New Century Fellowship can live as fully into its vision as God wants it to live. Syvoskia never stops dreaming about what the future could hold for this congregation and its mission. She brings her members alongside her with the gifts they already have, and she empowers them to use those gifts in meaningful ways. The people of New Century Fellowship are always looking for what God will show them next.

> *One of the comforting aspects of the Psalms is how the writers can envision God's deliverance in the midst of difficult circumstances. In Psalm 22, after the author cries about feeling forsaken. He ends his poem with, "Future generations will be told about the Lord and proclaim his deliverance to a people yet unborn, saying that he has done it" (v. 30–31). Mary picks up on that theme, singing a song of salvation in the future tense before the Messiah is even born (Luke 1:46–55). On the day of Pentecost, Peter quotes the prophet Joel when he preaches that God's people will have visions and dreams about the work Of God's Spirit (Acts 2:17–21). These examples and more are a reminder that God is doing a "new thing" in our midst if we have the eyes to see it and the ears to hear it (Is. 43:19).*

Texts for Study

- Genesis 32:22–29
- Psalm 22
- Acts 2:17–21

QUESTIONS FOR DISCUSSION AND REFLECTION

1. What attributes of your church's mission and vision encourage the congregation to be forward thinking?

2. What innovation outside of the church currently intrigues you? This might be in educational methods, the technology sector, healthcare, politics, etc. How can you adapt that innovation to work for your congregation?

3. What have you learned from other organizations in your community about being "on the move?"

4. Whom do you recognize as a potential leader in your congregation? What can you do to help them see themselves that way?

5. For congregations that are bound to a building, what does it look like to be a church on the move? How can you be "on the move, right where you are?"

Thriving Congregations
Refuse Be Stagnant

The Story of Beech Grove Christian Church, Beech Grove, Kentucky

It may seem incongruous that a chapter about how thriving congregations refuse to be stagnant features a church with a minister who's been there for a long time. If anything would nudge a minister and congregation toward complacency, it would be serving together for thirty-seven years. And, really, to what extent can congregation members resist stagnation when they've been hearing the same voice deliver sermons, offer prayers, and provide leadership for almost four decades?

In a big city or sprawling suburb, this may not be as salient an issue. As people move in and out of community, the makeup of the church changes, meaning the pastor is almost forced to help the congregation continually rediscover its identity and calling within its specific context. Programs and ministries change and adapt to meet the ever-changing needs of the congregation's members and community.

Beech Grove is not a big city or a sprawling suburb. Far from it. This unincorporated community tucked away in the western part of Kentucky claimed a population of 282 in the 2020 census. It's a half-hour drive from the city of Owensboro. The graduating class of the county high school is usually around a hundred students. There is just one stand-alone restaurant in town. And when a Dollar General Store was built nearby a few years ago, it was dubbed the "Beech Grove Mall." So, how does a church thrive in a community that's smaller than some churches' Sunday morning worship attendance?

Beech Grove Christian Church is a prime example of what it means to thrive in ways that defy the latest church growth literature. While experts in the field will tell you that thriving equals numerical growth, and numerical growth is attained through programs like small groups or intentional evangelism efforts, the leaders at Beech Grove have taken a different approach. They've listened to the needs of their congregation and community and adapted to meet them, creating an environment where change is desired and there's no such thing as a status quo.

It starts with the pastor, Rev. Jim Midkiff. When Jim came to Beech Grove in 1987, the congregation had a core family whose several siblings and grandchildren constituted about half of the congregation. There were a handful of other families in the church, and most of them were friends and neighbors, people who also spent time together outside of worship. While the town may not have changed much, Jim notes that this "wide spot in the road," as he endearingly calls it, "does things in a big way." The sense of community is strong, and the church enjoys a synergistic relationship with the residents of Beech Grove in a way that honors the culture and values while injecting a homegrown spirituality. For example, for the last fifteen years, the church has sponsored the "Blessing of the Hunt," when each November a bunch of hunters show up in their camo gear for a potluck dinner and pray for the safety of the hunters (and for bagging a big buck, Jim acknowledges).

When Jim came to Beech Grove, the church itself was in a good place, with about twenty youth, ranging from newborns to high schoolers, and an average worship attendance in the seventies. As the grandchildren started graduating and moving out, the church struggled to attract new members. Yet slowly but surely, new families started to move into this downtown church, which helped it grow bigger than the smaller churches that existed in the suburbs.

And yet Jim and the congregation don't see those other churches as competition, even when the pool of potential congregants is so small. The churches have, for the past 75+ years, held community Thanksgiving and Easter Sunrise services, alternating hosting churches, and with all ministers participating in the service. The area churches

Thriving Congregations Refuse Be Stagnant 125

collectively hosted a revival last summer, with each preacher taking a turn in the pulpit. "It's good for all of us," says Jim, whose laid-back preaching style was a stark contrast to the more conservative pastors from the other churches. "If I jumped up and shouted and yelled and talked really loud, my members would get up and leave," Jim says. "Our styles may be different, but we are serving the same Lord in the same community, and the members love the opportunities we have to come together."

People aren't leaving Beech Grove; in fact, just the opposite. The church experienced a surge of new members, with multiple families joining in the two-year period leading up to the pandemic. That time was a crisis for many churches, and Beech Grove was no different. A few families left, which hits harder in a smaller church. And yet Beech Grove soldiered on, staying true to its values while seeking to minister to those in their church family. Jim preached his weekly sermons from the table of his hundred-year-old father's kitchen, for whom Jim cared during the pandemic. The result of Jim's persistence in serving during that challenging time has been a sustained, faithful presence in a period when many smaller, rural churches are closing their doors. Now, Beech Grove has an average of sixty or so worshippers on Sundays, which swells to over a hundred or special Sundays—a third of the town's population.

But the impact of Beech Grove's ministry can't be confined to Sunday morning. One of the ways the church refuses to remain stagnant is being open to ministering to their community in ways that may not show up in an annual report, like providing a livestream of the worship services that usually generates around sixty weekly views. Another example is the annual fish fry the church hosts, which draws many folks from the community who aren't members. Jim tells the story of one attendee in his eighties who has expressed interest in Beech Grove but has yet to step foot in the sanctuary. Jim performed the funeral for this man's wife in 2023, and the man is still processing his grief. But there's a more practical reason for his non-attendance.

"He just can't hear very well," Jim says, noting that the man had recently lost his third set of hearing aids. But at the fish fry, the man

126　THRIVING CHURCH

told Jim, "I think I'm in good shape with the Lord. It's just nice to be around other Christians." He didn't show up at church the day after the fish fry, but Jim says, "Saturday night was good for him. I think he considers us his church, even though he didn't come."

Another way Beech Grove bucks the trend of what most people would consider to be a thriving church is that their minister has another job besides serving the church. Jim is bivocational, serving roughly ten to fifteen hours a week at the church along with his other job as a hospice chaplain. Jim lives about thirty minutes' drive from Beech Grove, which means he doesn't have any choice but to share leadership and ministry with the congregation. "Being bivocational, I knew I would need lots of help," Jim says.

That help has taken on a variety of forms, many of which demonstrate Beech Grove's willingness to think outside the box. Or, in some cases, the pulpit. Upon arriving at Beech Grove, it didn't take Jim long to realize that the demands the church was placing on him were more than he could handle. "After I had been there two years, I became overwhelmed with teaching at Ohio County Middle School, being a husband, being a father to two kids, and preaching," Jim says. Like many pastors, Jim was trying to juggle all the personal and vocational responsibilities and found that it was just too much. But unlike many pastors, Jim had the courage to raise his hand and ask for help.

Actually, his cry for help came in the form of his resignation. The timing coincided with the resignation of another pastor from a nearby Disciples church. That pastor, Brian Hedges, started filling in at Beech Grove. One night, Jim got a call from one of the leaders of Beech Grove. Jim recounts that the leader said, "We really like you as a minister. Brian has just been supply-preaching for you, and we really like him. We've been thinking, if you're both going to supply preach, why don't you both do it here?"

The church's response was not only unconventional, but it ensured the health of the church's leadership into the future. Jim and Brian preached alternating Sundays, filling in for each other as needed, and ensuring that Beech Grove had ministerial leadership. Jim asked a lay

Thriving Congregations Refuse Be Stagnant 127

leader, "What if we both preach on the same scripture one Sunday, not knowing the other one has preached on it?" The lay leader's wise response was, "We just get two different viewpoints." A situation that was increasingly untenable for Jim, and that would ultimately have negative consequences for the congregation was resolved because the church wasn't bound to the traditional way of doing things.

Can one church really be served effectively by two pastors? Surely this division of leadership created a rift in the congregation, right? Just the opposite. "We did this very effectively for twelve years," Jim says. He had two different co-pastors during that time (Brian served for four years and Maria Oliver for eight more), and only became the solo pastor again when his younger child was finishing high school. Jim's vulnerability and Beech Grove's willingness not to play by the rules turned a difficult situation into one in which both pastor and congregation could thrive.

Jim's approach to leadership was crucial to the success of the co-pastor model and has been a foundational element of Beech Grove's thriving. "I would describe Jim's leadership style as an encourager and servant leader," says lifelong church member Alita Reynolds. Jim's spiritual gift is encouraging, helping others to see the gifts in themselves and how they can live them out to the glory of God's kin-dom. "I make suggestions and encourage other to also, knowing there is no I' in Team," says Jim.

That collaborative approach to ministry helps Beech Grove avoid complacency. At a time when congregations are graying and struggling to remain relevant to younger generations, Beech Grove has put an emphasis on making disciples of younger generations. Some church folks see the youth as the "future of the church," but they can also use that platitude as a justification for not welcoming young people into leadership. It's easy to cast judgment and hold onto power when young people are not valued, ensuring that change is less likely to happen—and that the church will probably cease to exist a lot sooner.

At Beech Grove, the leaders not only talk the talk about supporting the youth, but they also live it out. Jim said that when he first started at Beech Grove, there was an active youth program with Sunday School, youth choirs, and regular outings. But youth ministry tends to be cyclical, and Beech Grove's population shifted to much younger youth. Jim recalls, "So, we started catering to that age," which includes a renewed emphasis on attending church camp. "Between our members and friends, we had 23 kids attend camp," Jim says. Recognizing the positive ripple effect that church camp attendance was having on the congregation, the church committed to raising money to help subsidize the cost of camp for families. The next summer, twenty-eight kids from Beech Grove went to church camp, and the church has now hired a former camper to start a youth group at Beech Grove.

This swell in youth attendance is indicative of Beech Grove's willingness to adapt in order to avoid stagnation. Many churches experiencing this kind of growth would expect new people to conform to the church's way of doing things. But Jim recognizes that the church exists to serve others and must be willing to break from past traditions and structures in order to stay relevant. This has included starting new Sunday School classes for kids and creating a social time in the fellowship hall for the parents.

To what does Jim attribute Beech Grove's refusal to be stagnant? "The open-mindedness of the congregation," he says. "We're a very joyful church." Alita adds, "We focus more on how we can help and be a servant in our church and community rather than growing members each Sunday and the money." The sense of community and willingness to serve its neighbors will keep Beech Grove vibrant into the future. Whether its inviting family resource coordinators from local schools to take the leftover clothes from the church's rummage sale or providing hotdogs and chili to families trick-or-treating on Halloween, Beech Grove is always looking for ways to shine Christ's light in their community, faithfully following wherever Christ calls them to serve this wide spot in the road in a big way.

Finding Identity

Congregations who are thriving might most easily be identified by their willingness to look carefully at who they are. Inevitably, this means the congregation is willing to consider that change might be in

Thriving Congregations Refuse Be Stagnant 129

their future. Like all institutions, congregations seek the status quo. They like stability and comfort. Stability breeds familiarity, which, in contrast to the adage, breeds fondness. Aside from new church starts, almost every congregation has members who refer to the church "as it used to be" or talk in meetings of "how we've always done" something. However, when a congregation is willing to do the introspective work to discover their mission—who God is calling them to be at this time and in this place—they're also willing to admit when changes need to occur.

In the case of Beech Grove, the congregation sees change as exciting. For this congregation in the tiny town for whom the church is named, change is something that keeps the congregation vibrant. For larger congregations, or for congregations with a constant influx and outflow of members, change happens organically. New voices bring new idea. But in Beech Grove, the congregants are constant. They see very little change in their core membership, aside from people added to the already existing families. And yet, they seek out new ways to be church together.

So, what breeds this? What makes Beech Grove a unique place? We argue that there is nothing inherently different about the structure of this rural church with a bivocational pastor; rather, the difference is the constant recentering on creative ways to engage their community. Beech Grove functions just like most churches with congregational governance. The church has a board, elders and deacons, business meetings, and governing documents just like most churches. The difference for Beech Grove is its willingness to be creative and embrace change.

For example, thriving churches don't look at their mission once every ten years and update the language to say the exact same thing in more time-conscious language. They don't just remove the gendered pronouns and call it good enough. Thriving churches view their mission as an extension of themselves—indeed a core part that needs frequent nurture and attention. In order to resist the status quo and be willing to change, congregations have to do deep work to understand their context. They must know who is moving into town, who is moving

130 · THRIVING CHURCH

out of town, and who is burdened by the systemic forces unique to their geographic location. Churches who are most willing to do this are those for whom change is easiest. That's what Beech Grove does. Its people return to their calling and ask themselves, "What does God want us to be doing now?" This "wide spot in the road" makes a big impact by continuing to ask what God is up to in their little town.

When you know the people around you—really know them—you begin to see your church differently. Beech Grove is a congregation that knows its community. Because this church pays attention to its neighbors, it knows that most folks in its community have needs that may initially not be obvious. Serving chili and hotdogs on Halloween is more than a way to remind their town of the church's presence; it's also a way to provide a hot meal and a full helping of hospitality to families who need it. Changing the age focus of the youth group is a recognition that few high schoolers were present in their church at the time. Providing a time of fellowship for parents during youth Sunday School enables siloed friends an opportunity to reconnect. The church which refuses to be stagnant is continually looking for its new identity.

What about the Naysayers?

Every church has a few folks whose favorite word seems to be "No." It may be voiced as "That won't work," or "I have my doubts" sometimes, but whatever the exact language, ultimately the response is "No." How does a congregation bring those folks along to "I'll give it a chance"? It depends on relationships. Rather than just saying, "Well, Linda isn't going to like that," congregations like Beech Grove are eager to say, "I have a really good relationship with Linda. Let me see if I can understand her concerns." Sometimes what these churches find is that Linda has deeply personal reasons for why she says no. Spending time hearing her story enables the congregation to tend to her needs pastorally while also moving forward.

For example, perhaps a church is considering re-writing the mission statement. Linda might be saying, "That mission statement has been here my entire life; we don't need to change it! It defines us." When Linda's good friend Janice invites her to coffee to talk about it, Janice discovers that Linda's dad was the church treasurer when that mission statement was written. Perhaps Linda didn't even realize that she is hanging on to that mission statement because of how it connected her to her father, or maybe she did, but the conversation with Janice allows her to say aloud, in a trusted space, why the thought of changing the statement is grieving her. Janice, in turn, has the opportunity to say, "And your father was a vital part of making sure our church stayed relevant to the community in his time. We have had such gifted and giving leadership throughout our history. This could be our legacy for our kids and grandkids." Linda may never like the new mission statement, but when the statement is approved and is displayed on the wall, she knows that her dad's work has not been forgotten. Her relationship with Janice has helped her to be a more informed member of her church community. She feels seen and understood. And she knows that the mission statement isn't changing just for the sake of change. Instead, she knows that the time of her father's leadership was different from the time now, and she can recognize why a new statement is important.

Death and Resurrection

Part of change means laying to rest some of the things we love. With varying degrees of mourning, congregations have set aside programs and ministries. And yet churches still resist allowing something good to die. Just because a ministry is good doesn't mean it's necessary.

Perhaps your congregation has held a holiday bazaar for the last twenty years as a fundraiser for the congregation's mission efforts. Members of the church spend months crafting and gluing, stitching and sewing, making items for the public to purchase. All the supplies are donated, and the profits are how the church funds its outreach. But the people who make the crafts now have arthritis and dementia and fatigue. They're caring for aging siblings and spouses. They deeply love the bazaar and want to see the church's mission efforts be well-funded, but they just can't make as many things as they used to. Younger artisans are not joining the bazaar project, even those gifted with the necessary skills.

132   THRIVING CHURCH

Allowing the bazaar to be in hospice care and to pass away is not to say that the bazaar has been meaningless. Consider how awful it would be to say to a grieving person whose spouse is in hospice, "Just give it up! No one is going to miss her!" The same is true of a ministry or program that needs to die. Congregations should *never* diminish the impact a ministry has had on the community or on the lives of those who participated in it. Rather, the ministry should be celebrated; churches should speak of the bazaar as a great gift that twenty years of faithful members gave to the church and the community through their tireless work. Perhaps the final bazaar could be a celebration of bazaars of the past—recreating crafts of which you have images, or framing pictures of the original creators of the bazaar! Allow the ministry that needs to die to die. But never let it be forgotten.

In the case of Beech Grove, the congregation participated in a regional, mission-focused project called Surfing the Edge that encouraged congregations to designate money to missions in their area. To this day—at least a decade later—the congregation still has a Surfing the Edge Fund on its books that is designated for urgent needs in their community. The congregation no longer participates in the program, but the program changed the way the church manages its funds and its namesake lives on. For many at Beech Grove, referencing the fund recalls a significant time of transformation in the life of the church. The congregation now encourages its children and youth to find the ministry needs in their schools and bring them to the church as opportunities to share their resources. The impact of Surfing the Edge is still a vital part of this church's identity, even if the program itself is long gone.

Engaging New Voices

The Surfing the Edge Fund meets essential needs like paying utility bills, but it also funds things like new shoes for a child who wants to play on the school basketball team. The church has learned to trust their children and youth about the needs they see around them. Furthermore, they have trained these same kids to notice needs and speak to their church about it. Children and youth at Beech Grove are not the future of the church, they're active and engaged members of the congregation *now*.

Thriving Congregations Refuse Be Stagnant 133

For some congregations, this is the defining challenge: allowing new voices to shape the conversation. Whether it is Beech Grove charging their young people to find the needs in the community or your church inviting your newest members to sit on the Board, a thriving church refuses to be stagnant by engaging new voices. Who in your congregation has a voice? Whose voice is missing? When you look across the congregation, are all of the segments of your church represented in the decision makers? If not, the best way to avoid stagnation is to bring in those voices.

Imagine for a moment your church building. If you had never been inside that building, would you know where to find the restroom or the nursery? How would you know this church's particular ways of taking communion? When a church invites new voices into positions of leadership (formal and informal), it finds out the answers to these questions. When churches struggle to relinquish their structures of influence and power, they miss the opportunity to see the world and the church through fresh eyes. Finding ways to keep a congregation moving forward almost always includes listening to those who are often overlooked. If a pastor of thirty-seven years can do it, so can your church.

> *Throughout the First Testament, God calls people to be on the move. Frequently people are called from their places of comfort into new and strange lands for a variety of reasons. Sometimes God calls them to protect them from danger, sometimes as a promise of providence in a new place. In the Gospels, Jesus is always on the move. The church which refuses to be stagnant may not move its physical location as often as these faithful people, but the mindset of the thriving church is to ask, "Where is God calling us to go now?"*

Texts to Study

- Genesis 28:10–22
- Ruth 1:7–22
- Matthew 4:12–23

QUESTIONS FOR REFLECTION AND DISCUSSION

1. Why do you think we included Genesis 28:10–22 in a chapter on refusing to be stagnant? What does Jacob's dream have to say to your church about this work?

2. How does your church answer the question "What is God up to now?" How do you determine the answers to that question?

3. In what areas of ministry does your church currently run the risk of stagnating? What programs/ministries/activities have already stagnated or are nearing stagnation?

4. How does your church already resist stagnation? What can you do to encourage your church to be a people on the move?

5. In Matthew 4, Jesus calls his first disciples, and they immediately leave their fishing nets to follow Jesus. These disciples are mirroring what Jesus does in verse 13. What can your church learn from Jesus in this passage?

Conclusion

The Story of Your Congregation

As you can see from these stories, thriving congregations come in all shapes, sizes, colors, and stages of existence. And yet, in the midst of the diversity, they have aspects of congregational life in common. We hope these stories have helped you imagine what thriving looks like in your own congregation. Let us offer you one final metaphor for envisioning your community of faith as a thriving congregation.

Lessons from a Tree

Thriving churches can be described as trees. They are rooted, they have a solid trunk, and their branches stay well-pruned to bear good fruit. Consider the elements of a tree as you think about the things your church might need to thrive.

Roots

We began these stories with the chapter entitled *Thriving Congregations are Rooted in Scripture* because we believe that is where a church finds its nourishment. Roots serve two purposes: nourishment and stability. The root system of a tree often mirrors the shape of the branches, providing balance and support. As the tree grows, so too do the roots, always reaching deeper and further into the soil to ensure the tree has what it needs to flourish. So too does the thriving church dig deeper and further into scripture to find its nourishment and support. Perhaps the single most important thing a church can do if it wants to enrich its thriving is to spend intentional time rooting itself in the scripture and finding its particular story in the wider story of

God's people. From there, it will find what it needs for the church to flourish. While these roots may not be readily visible, they provide stability. Rather than following the latest trends, a thriving church is solidly anchored in God's word and has the freedom to live it out in its own context.

Trunk

All of the traits of a thriving church you find in this book can be related back to the trunk: *Thriving Congregations Understand their Mission and Vision.* The mission and vision are the means by which all of the other traits find their grounding in scripture. To have a deep understanding of scripture but no sense of purpose means that your other traits cannot flourish. Churches need a mission, and they find that mission by rooting themselves in the scriptures. The nourishment, encouragement, strength, and sustenance that come from the scriptures, coupled with the question. "What is God calling us to do/be in this time and this place?" will help your congregation to bear good fruit. By following that mission, the church delivers the life-giving nutrients of scripture to the various thriving branches. Like a tree trunk, the mission connects the story rooted in scripture to the stories being lived out through the traits.

Branches

The other eight traits we have explored in this book can be considered the branches of the tree. When a church is rooted in scripture and understands who or what it is called to be, it is free to explore what it means to be a risk-taking congregation, a flexible church, a church which rejects fear, a church which collaborates, and so on. The work of the thriving church manifests itself in the branches. This is the part of the tree that most people will notice. They see the unique pattern, the colorful leaves, the animals that take shelter in the branches and trunk and under the bark, and they know what kind of tree it is. The same is true of the church: people will see these traits in you and will know what kind of church to expect when they walk through your doors.

Conclusion 137

Fruit

Healthy trees bear fruit. They produce seeds or pinecones or stone fruits or berries or nuts—whatever fruit is unique to its species. Fruit nourishes the lives of those around it—the animals, the birds, the pollinators, the insects, and the people. Every species of tree bears different fruit for a different purpose. Because your tree bears apples and another tree bears maple seeds does not mean that one tree is thriving better than the other; it simply means the trees have different purposes. The same is true of the church. When your church is rooted in scripture, knows its mission, and allows its branches to bear fruit, it will nourish those around you.

Finally, a tree bears fruit and seeds to reproduce. The flourishing tree desires to spread and to create new versions of itself. Not all churches desire to plant new congregations, but we hope that all churches want to spread the good news to fresh soil.

Pruning

Trees need to be pruned. Arborists recommend that trees be pruned every few years, depending on the species and maturity of the tree. Tending to your congregation's thriving is not a "one and done" act; it requires attention over the years to be sure you are still growing in the ways that God wants you to grow. We hope that as your congregation finds new depths of thriving, you will also develop a rhythm of pruning. Tend to your vision, nurture the gifts within your congregation to develop deeper traits, explore where God is leading you next as the culture around you shifts and return to the scriptures to grow new roots.

Conclusion

Thriving congregations exist not because of some magic formula but because of their commitment to follow God's calling for them. We hope this book has given you the opportunity to see the ways in which your congregation is already thriving and to hear stories of churches that are doing that in unique ways. Our prayer is that you continue to live into who God is calling you to be, thriving in ways that shine God's light and love in this world, which so desperately needs exactly what you have to give. May what you have learned in these pages be the spark for the next chapter of your own church's story!